Rethinking US Education Policy

# Rethinking US Education Policy

## Paradigms of the Knowledge Economy

*Daniel Araya*

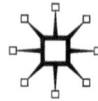

RETHINKING US EDUCATION POLICY
Copyright © Daniel Araya, 2015.

All rights reserved.

First published in 2015 by
PALGRAVE MACMILLAN®
in the United States—a division of St. Martin's Press LLC,
175 Fifth Avenue, New York, NY 10010.

Where this book is distributed in the UK, Europe and the rest of the world, this is by Palgrave Macmillan, a division of Macmillan Publishers Limited, registered in England, company number 785998, of Houndmills, Basingstoke, Hampshire RG21 6XS.

Palgrave Macmillan is the global academic imprint of the above companies and has companies and representatives throughout the world.

Palgrave® and Macmillan® are registered trademarks in the United States, the United Kingdom, Europe and other countries.

ISBN: 978–1–137–47555–8

Library of Congress Cataloging-in-Publication Data

Araya, Daniel, 1971–
    Rethinking US education policy : paradigms of the knowledge economy / Daniel Araya.
        pages cm
    Includes bibliographical references and index.
    ISBN 978–1–137–47555–8 (hardback)
        1. Education and state—United States. I. Title.
LC89.A817 2015
379.73—dc23                                                          2014042661

A catalogue record of the book is available from the British Library.

Design by Newgen Knowledge Works (P) Ltd., Chennai, India.

First edition: May 2015

10 9 8 7 6 5 4 3 2 1

For my Mother and Father, in thanks for their love and support

# Contents

*List of Illustrations* ix
*Foreword* xi
*Abbreviations and Acronyms* xv

Introduction 1
1  US Education Policy as Economic Policy 17
2  The Knowledge Economy in Context 31
3  Paradigms of the Knowledge Economy 51
4  Education Policy and the Obama Administration 77
5  The Knowledge Economy in Dialogue 107
6  Rethinking US Education Policy 137

*Notes* 155
*Bibliography* 161
*Index* 179

# Illustrations

## Figures

| | | |
|---|---|---|
| 0.1 | The smiling curve | 2 |
| 4.1 | US innovation strategy | 81 |
| 6.1 | New STEM professions through 2020 | 140 |

## Tables

| | | |
|---|---|---|
| 0.1 | The grammar of schooling | 7 |
| 0.2 | Working premises | 13 |
| 2.1 | Definitions of NIS | 43 |
| 3.1 | Multiple discourses on the Knowledge Economy | 52 |
| 3.2 | Four paradigms of the Knowledge Economy | 53 |
| 4.1 | Strategy for American innovation | 84 |
| 4.2 | Actual ARRA spending during the period 2009–2011 (in billions) | 86 |
| 4.3 | Total ARRA funds for education (in billions) | 87 |
| 5.1 | Four paradigms of the Knowledge Economy | 109 |
| 6.1 | Models of political economy | 147 |

# Foreword

In his address at Georgetown University in April 2009, President Obama introduced five public policy pillars as a foundation to rebuilding the economy and society of the United States. Responding to the recent collapse of the US economy under the weight of a frenzied capital market, the new president emphasized new rules that he believed would stem the economic contagion that had begun to spread globally. These pillars included: new rules for Wall Street, including greater regulation of finance capitalism; increased investment in education at all levels in the preparation of students for the twenty-first century; promotion and investment in clean energy technologies designed to utilize renewable resources; reform of the US health care system in order to curb inflated costs and advance universal health care provision; and reduction of the deficit in the creation of a sustainable economic future.

According to President Obama, these five pillars would serve as the basis upon which the US economy could rebuild in order to ensure long-term economic sustainability. Making a case for "change," the new president had signaled a deliberate move away from the speculative bubble of unregulated neoliberal finance capitalism and toward a system with greater checks and balances. Now five years on—at the close of President Obama's second term—the obvious question is what has been the impact of these policies? On balance, many would argue that some of these policies have been successful while others have not. The United States now appears to be in recovery, despite a widespread concern about long-term social and economic inequality, and a rising anxiety about a future characterized by a kind of oligarchic capitalism.

At the same time, developed countries are now increasingly under pressure to produce public policies that leverage high rates of innovation to sustain economic growth. Since the 1990s, economic strategies on innovation in the United States and other countries have been constructed around a multifaceted discourse on globalization promoted by world policy organizations such as the Organisation for Economic Co-operation and Development (OECD) and the World Bank. Public policies focusing on the move from a mass industrial economy to a postindustrial economy have called attention to the production and consumption of knowledge and symbolic goods as the defining feature of our time. In the field of education policy, for example, most theorists agree that the epochal nature of this deep economic transformation now calls for a significant rethinking on education.

In my own work I have tried to distinguish between a number of different strands and readings of the knowledge economy in order to provide a history of the policies and theories that now cluster around ideas of a postindustrial society. I have outlined the different strands of this discourse and attempted to theorise not only knowledge economy but also the parallel term "knowledge society" in an attempt to relate these terms to wider and broader changes in the nature of capitalism and the global economy. As I have suggested, the evolution of the discourse on knowledge economy often reflects contradictory or opposing ideological sources with unique histories and visions of the economy and society. I have argued that "knowledge economy" or "knowledge society" are not simply neoliberal notions but are predicated on a complex and openly contested policy landscape.

Building on my work, Daniel Araya has framed these strands as paradigms of knowledge economy with a similar interest in charting the trajectory of these policies for US education. In this book, Araya explores the latest concepts and theories of postindustralism in order to discuss four specific paradigms of the knowledge economy and their implications for shaping US education under the Obama administration. Exploring the Neoliberal Knowledge Economy; the Network Economy; the Creative Economy; and the Green Economy, Araya articulates policy scenarios that build on these vastly different readings of postindustrial society.

In fact, these four paradigms represent the dominant conceptions of economy in the now mainstream literature promoting the policy futures for education in the twenty-first century. In articulating these policy scenarios for US education policy, Araya draws on the tradition of critical educational policy scholarship to develop a post-neoliberal conception of US education. This is an interesting set of moves that charts the fundamental paradox that education has transitioned from its welfare, equality and social cohesion roles under classical liberalism to an economic good under neoliberalism and part of the central machinery of the innovation economy. The neoliberal transformation of education is almost complete and seemingly impossible to reverse in terms of piece-meal policy-making. The significance of these changes is perhaps greatest and most keenly felt in the growth of student tuition fees and loans in the US to well over a trillion dollars. Education has become the latest growth dimension of global finance capitalism that mortgages student futures and the next generation of "human capital."

What in fact the neoliberal era has encouraged is a transformation of the Fordist welfare state of industrial capitalism into the postindustrial competition state of corporatized capitalism. This policy constellation reflects the dominant influence of neoliberalism and financialization of a market society under the authority of the "financial class" so-called Anglo-American capitalism. Building a case against the continued influence of Anglo-American capitalism, Araya surveys educational policy and planning generated under the Obama Administration and offers a compelling analysis of its failings.

Araya is an astute commentator as he reviews recent policy documents focusing on the National Economic Council's (2011) *A strategy for American innovation: Securing Our economic growth and prosperity*; the US Department of Education's (2010) *A blueprint for reform: The reauthorization of the elementary and secondary education act*; and US Department of Education's (2010) *Transforming American education: Learning powered by technology, national education technology plan*. The resulting analysis is a powerful and compelling picture and critique of US education within the global economy.

In chapter 5, Araya supplements this documentary analysis with interviews of some of the most expert thinkers including the likes of Richard Florida, Michel Bauwens and Sam Pitroda. One of the most valuable services that the book provides is the framework for rethinking US educational policy beyond superficial and precipitous readings. Most importantly, he explores the political economy of education in search of an alternative framework for guiding US education policy in the twenty-first century. Political economy has a disciplinary past that reaches back into the Enlightenment, but unlike traditional economics, it emphasizes questions of social justice and legitimate government in relation to the production, distribution, and exchange of goods and services. In this vein, *Rethinking US Education Policy* seeks to build on this intellectual heritage with a special emphasis on the political economy of education. In truth, education has always been understood as part of political economy, not merely in terms of "alienated labor" or the "wealth of nations" but in relation to how societies construct their own intersubjectivity and capacities for self-overcoming.

This book represents the culmination of Araya's dissertation work while at the University of Illinois at Urbana-Champaign. I was fortunate to act as his advisor and clearly remember the often-heated discussions we had as colleagues over the concepts and theories (as only those who care deeply about their work do). In the interim, Daniel completed several edited books collaborating with me on related aspects of knowledge economy. He was a quick learner and soon had initiated collaborations and edited collections of his own.

While this represents Araya's thinking on the future of US education policy, my suggestion would be to read this in conjunction with his other works that deal in greater depth with aspects of his analysis. It is also apparent that he has gone beyond his earlier work to investigate the new technologies of openness and their potential for transforming education and economic and cultural development. It is with the greatest personal delight that I can heartily recommend this book.

MICHAEL A. PETERS
Professor, University of Waikato, New Zealand
Professor Emeritus, University of Illinois at
Urbana-Champaign, United States

# Abbreviations and Acronyms

| | |
|---|---|
| AI | Artificial Intelligence |
| ANAR | A Nation At Risk |
| ARPA-E | Advanced Research Projects Agency Energy |
| ARPA-ED | Advanced Research Projects Agency Education |
| ARRA | American Recovery and Reinvestment Act |
| BFR | Blueprint for Reform |
| BRIC | Brazil, Russia, India, China |
| CCS | Common Core State Standards |
| CCSSI | Common Core State Standards Initiative |
| CCSO | Council of Chief State School Officers |
| CE | Creative Economy |
| COMPETES | Creating Opportunities to Meaningfully Promote Excellence in Technology, Education, and Science |
| DARPA | Defense Advanced Research Projects Agency |
| DER | Distributed Energy Resources |
| DOE | Department of Energy |
| ESEA | Elementary and Secondary Education Act |
| EGT | Endogenous Growth Theory |
| EFRC | Energy Frontier Research Centers |
| EU | European Union |
| FDI | Foreign Direct Investment |
| FOSS | Free and Open Source Software |
| GE | Green Economy |
| GDP | Gross Domestic Product |
| GPS | Global Positioning Satellite |
| HC | Human Capital |
| HCT | Human Capital Theory |
| ICT | Information and Communication Technology |
| IGO | Intergovernmental Organization |

| | |
|---|---|
| IMF | International Monetary Fund |
| IP | Intellectual Property |
| IT | Information Technology |
| JOLTS | Job Opening and Labor Turnover Survey |
| K-12 | Kindergarten-Grade 12 |
| KBC | Knowledge-based Capital |
| KE | Knowledge Economy |
| LLL | Lifelong Learning |
| M2M | Machine-to-Machine |
| NASA | National Aeronautical Space Agency |
| NCLB | No Child Left Behind |
| NEPC | National Education Policy Center |
| NE | Network Economy |
| NETP | National Educational Technology Plan |
| NGA | National Governors Association |
| NIEs | Newly Industrialized Economies |
| NIS | National Innovation System |
| NSF | National Science Foundation |
| OA | Open Access |
| OAC | Open Access Coalition |
| OCW | Open Courseware |
| ODL | Open and Distance Learning |
| OE | Open Education |
| OECD | Organization for Economic Cooperation and Development |
| OER | Open Educational Resources |
| OS | Open Source |
| OSM | Open Source Movement |
| P2P | Peer to Peer |
| PISA | Program for International Student Assessment |
| R&D | Research and Development |
| RTTT | Race to the Top |
| SBIR | Small Business Innovation Research Program |
| SBTC | Skill-biased Technological Change |
| STEM | Science, Technology, Engineering and Math |
| SAI | Strategy for American Innovation |
| TARP | Troubled Asset Relief Program |
| TIMSS | Trends in International Mathematics and Science Study |

| | |
|---|---|
| TWG | Technical Working Group |
| UK | United Kingdom |
| UN | United Nations |
| UNESCO | United Nations Educational, Scientific and Cultural Organization |
| UNICEF | United Nations Children's Fund |
| UNCTAD | United Nations Conference on Trade and Development |
| US | United States |
| USDOE | US Department of Education |
| WB | World Bank |
| WIPO | World Intellectual Property Organization |
| WTO | World Trade Organization |

# Introduction

## Education for Innovation

It is no coincidence that the rising demand for higher education has developed in parallel with the expansion of a "knowledge economy" (KE). As the Organization for Economic Cooperation and Development (OECD, 1997) suggests, economic activities are now closely linked to education. Innovation-driven economies are said to be dependent upon smooth flows of knowledge (both tacit and codified) and investments in "adoption capability" (or the knowledge embodied in skilled labor as "human capital"). Put simply, investments in human capital augment skilled labor my making skilled workers more productive. (Goldin & Katz, 2008; Acemoglu & Autor, 2012).

Accelerating trends in economic philosophy now explicitly link investments in education and training to economic performance (Becker, 1964, 1975) because "thick profits" are said to be concentrated in industries that require higher-level skills and abilities (figure 0.1).

Beyond the era of mass production, human capital theory is now viewed as a critical instrument in the development of social policy in OECD countries. Indeed, investments in human capital are seen as key to mitigating "skill-biased technological change" (SBTC). Building on human capital theory, SBTC is understood as a long-term shift that favors skilled over unskilled labor by increasing labor's relative productivity and therefore its relative demand (Katz, 1999). As KE stimulates rising skill premiums, so growing demand for human capital elevates the value of higher education.

Studies indicate that the diffusion of information and communication technologies (ICTs) in the workplace has only intensified SBTC (Spitz, 2004). ICTs are seen as complementary to skilled

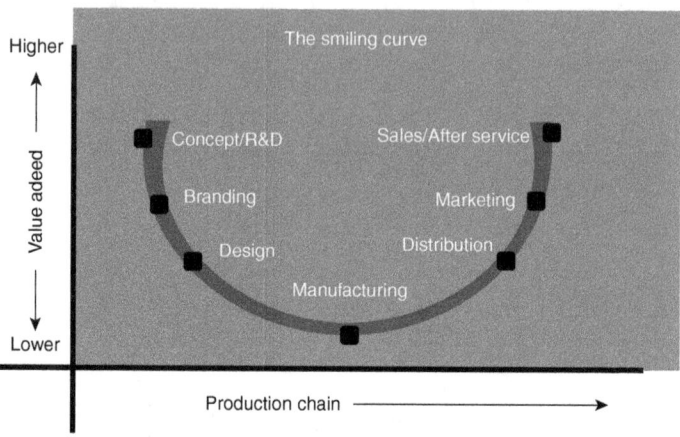

**Figure 0.1** The smiling curve.
Source: Adapted from Marber (2013, p. 30).

labor (at least in their adoption phase), and place "factor bias" at the center of the income-distribution debate (Piketty & Saez, 2012; Piketty, 2014; Violante, 2014).

The long-term consequence of SBTC, however, is that *underemployment* has become a serious problem. In the United States, 25 million households (the bottom fifth of the income ladder) now earn $18,000 or less annually (Kenworthy, 2014). Adjusting for inflation, wages in the United States have not increased since the mid-1970s. In fact, recent data from the US Bureau of Labor Statistics (2014) indicate that civilian labor force participation has been declining since 2009.

> Over the past three decades, labour's share of output has shrunk globally from 64% to 59%. Meanwhile, the share of income going to the top 1% in America has risen from around 9% in the 1970s to 22% today. Unemployment is at alarming levels in much of the rich world, and not just for cyclical reasons. In 2000, 65% of working-age Americans were in work; since then the proportion has fallen, during good years as well as bad, to the current level of 59%. (*Economist*, 2014)

While policymakers in OECD countries have tended to focus on rising competition from developing countries, the reality is that something even more fundamental is transforming the global economy. Indeed, advances in technological innovation are introducing massive changes across the political and economic landscape. Between 1995 and 2002, 22 million manufacturing jobs were eliminated globally even as total production increased by 30 percent (Rifkin, 2014, p. 124). In fact, a recent study by the Oxford Martin School suggests that nearly half of all occupations in the United States could be displaced through technological automation over the next two decades (Frey & Osborne, 2013).

Massachusetts Institute of Technology economists Brynjolfsson and McAfee (2014) point out that technological automation has become a daunting challenge. In their book, *The Second Machine Age*, they highlight the dramatic evolution of ICTs and describe the magnitude of this technological revolution. They argue that the advance of ICTs is displacing human labor across multiple sectors of the global labor force and moving postindustrial society into a new era of automation.

What is especially perplexing about this economic restructuring is that productivity gains appear to be decoupling from jobs and income (even as new wealth is overwhelmingly consumed by the owners of capital). Notwithstanding the fact that the principle of workplace automation has not fundamentally changed since the dawn of the computer era, the costs of automation have in fact fallen dramatically. Exponential decline in computing costs has in turn fueled an ever-expanding substitution of fixed capital (computers) for labor. Indeed, while the speed of computing (per unit cost) doubled every three years between 1910 and 1950, and doubled every two years between 1950 and 1966, computing capacity at present is doubling every year (Autor, 2014).[1]

In contrast to the perception that it is only low-skilled labor that is most vulnerable to automation, theories on technological unemployment now argue just the opposite. According to Moravec's paradox, it is in fact *knowledge-based* labor that is most vulnerable to computerization. The reason for this is quite simple. Cognitive work that is based on precise, well-understood procedures is now easily codified and performed by machines, even as some factory automation remains specialized and expensive (Moravec, 1988; Brynjolfsson & McAfee, 2014).

## The Daunting Challenge of Educational Reform

Brynjolfsson and McAfee are not the first economists to suggest that technological innovation is linked to underemployment and rising inequality. It was the economist John Maynard Keynes who first coined the term "technological unemployment" to describe what he foresaw as the coming mass displacement of workers by machines. What is perhaps most surprising about today's computational revolution, however, is its expanding reach. Building on the combined power of digitization, exponential technological change, and recombinant innovation, computational technologies may soon be capable of displacing large segments of the labor force altogether. Beyond routine tasks, computers are becoming increasingly adept at higher cognitive functions including language processing, data analysis, and computer control systems.

Where OECD (2013) countries have emphasized the need for promoting competitive proficiencies overlapping advanced skills in literacy, numeracy, and problem-solving, one wonders whether this kind of skills-based training will be sufficient to overcome the challenges of technological innovation. Notwithstanding the fact that returns on investments in education have been substantial to US economic growth (Goldin & Katz, 2008), new data points to significant social challenges ahead. The obvious question today is what should education policy do to respond to technological automation. Even as student debt in the United States has surpassed one trillion dollars, a growing body of literature has called into question many of the central assumptions driving contemporary educational reform.

Building on a long history of innovation strategy (Freeman, 1987, 1995; Lundvall, 1992), education has traditionally been seen as an engine of development, reinforcing long-term investments in high-value goods and services. Today, however, mounting demand to augment human capital for KE has triggered a wide-ranging debate about the kinds of skills and competencies needed to drive OECD countries (Lundvall & Johnson, 1994; OECD, 1996). In truth, even as vocational training in science, technology, engineering, and math (STEM) has emerged as a common policy framework in the United States, tuition costs have now begun to outpace inflation.

The rise of new economic players across industries and shifts in the kinds of competitive skills and capabilities needed to advance postindustrial societies, have focused considerable media attention on education (Lundvall & Johnson, 1994). At the same time, widely varied forecasts on the future of postindustrial society demonstrate that reforming education is proving to be a daunting task. Where Brynjolfsson and McAfee advocate the redesign of schooling in correspondence to exponentially advancing technologies, others suggest that the scale of changes ahead may well outstrip the need for human labor altogether. Given growing income inequality and rising unemployment across multiple sectors of the labor force, many wonder whether this is a harbinger of more extreme economic polarization to come (Ghose, Majid, & Ernst, 2009).

Rifkin (2014), for example, argues against the common rhetoric on STEM training as a means to mitigate unemployment. In his estimation, technological change is not merely outpacing human labor, but the market dynamics of capitalism itself. Laying out the paradoxical consequences of Moore's law (i.e., the exponential growth of digital technologies), he suggests that the repercussions of digital technologies include a precipitous decline in the value of market economies for managing goods and services:

> The wholesale substitution of intelligent technology for mass labor and salaried professional labor is beginning to disrupt the workings of the capitalist system. The question economists are so fearful to entertain is, what happens to market capitalism when productivity gains, brought on by intelligent technology, continue to reduce the need for human labor? What we are seeing is the unbundling of productivity from employment. Instead of the former facilitating the latter, it is now eliminating it. (p. 132)

According to Rifkin, we are entering a post-market era in which schooling will become increasingly disconnected from productivity. Focusing on the decline of marginal costs due to accelerating computational technologies, he concludes that the slow unraveling of the profit rate is forcing capitalist societies to restructure around a commons-driven network society. Advancing on a convergence of exponentially evolving technologies (i.e., distributed green energy, artificial intelligence and robotics, 3D printing, and Internet-driven logistics), he argues that this new era will be configured around social collaboration and laterally scaling networks.

## Rethinking US Education Policy

Mounting interest in rejuvenating education systems in support of advanced skills and capabilities suggest the need for substantial investments in transforming bureaucratic and stratified systems of schooling. Advancing on this debate, the central argument of this book is that contemporary US educational reform policies are based upon contradictory readings of the knowledge economy. What is obvious, for example, is that advanced industrialized societies are entering an era in which many kinds of labor are becoming much less valuable.

Despite a growing recognition of the need for reform in education, much of the educational reform discourse misreads the changes associated with KE. While the main policy response to KE has been to focus on leveraging formal education to advance vocational skills, one wonders whether this really makes sense. As technology becomes increasingly democratized, formal schooling built for the industrial era may well be incompatible to the needs of knowledge-based societies.

Just as the first high schools in the United States emerged in response to the socioeconomic needs of a nineteenth-century industrial society, so today it is suggested that schooling should be retrofitted to the needs of a twenty-first-century postindustrial society.[2] The truth is that educational reform is now married to widely varied assumptions about the nature and function of schooling for KE. Perhaps the most prominent assumption is that formal education must now be retooled in correspondence to market-based logics (Slaughter & Leslie, 1997; Aronowitz, 2000; Slaughter & Rhoades, 2004). Indeed, the discussion around US educational reform assumes that the primary challenge facing education today is related to efficiency and cost. Rather than simply a problem of cost, I suggest that the real challenge facing US education today is related to quality and fit.

Waks (2013), for example, offers a pointed critique of the shallowness of contemporary US educational reform and the need to move beyond "factory schooling". As he points out, schools have long been organized in parallel with the centralized hierarchy found within the industrial factory. Indeed, the "first American high school was established in Boston in 1821, just as the first American mechanized factory was established in the same place" (p. 33). In truth, the US high school was a direct response to the need for both skilled manual labor and an evolving managerial class. Conveying students into a highly articulated industrial order, the overarching theme of factory schools has been that of "adjusting means to ends": improving efficiency (measured in terms of the ratio of predetermined ends per unit of input) and driving assessment by and through "egg-cart" classrooms. Tyack and Tobin (1994), for example, have described this didactic instructional system as the "grammar of schooling" (table 0.1).

As Waks (2013) points out, simply retrofitting factory schools with ICTs is not a solution. Indeed, new technologies embody inherent logics that require a rethinking of institutions and social practices. Beyond conventional transmission schooling built for the industrial age, ICTs reflect a new era with very different capabilities and affordances (Blinder, 2008). Beyond educational factories designed to *batch-process* knowledge transmission, the challenge today is to rethink the design and purpose of education altogether.

Notwithstanding narrow and often monolithic readings of KE, there remain open questions about the purpose of education in the

Table 0.1   The grammar of schooling

- Students organized in roughly identical "egg-crate" classrooms (radiating out from central corridors)
- A certified professional teacher in each classroom dispensing official instruction
- Standard, predetermined subject matter content, analyzed into goals, objectives, and competencies, generally supported by a textbook
- Didactic instructional methods, chiefly lecture-discussions and seat-work on prepared worksheets
- Assessment of learning by periodic subject matter tests based primarily upon memory and application of standard subject matter
- Education as "social reproduction," facilitating learning of basic academic skills and disciplines (often in support of sorting for stratified occupational roles)

*Source*: Adapted from Waks (2013, p. 38).

twenty-first century. The truth is that it has become commonplace to interpret educational reform policy in terms of rudimentary definitions of KE. Taken as a whole, the policy rhetoric on KE forms a kind of conceptual prism through which educational policy discourses are largely refracted. Indeed, the main goal of this book is to unpack these discourses in order to rethink US education policy.

Advancing on the work of Peters (2009a, 2010), this book explores four discourses or "paradigms" of KE and considers their influence in shaping US educational policy reform. These paradigms of KE include:

- The "Network Economy," as articulated by Yochai Benkler (2006), Axel Bruns (2008), Michel Bauwens (2006), and others.
- The "Creative Economy," as articulated by Richard Florida (2002a), Charles Landry (2000), and John Howkins (2001).
- The "Green Economy," as articulated by Brian Milani (2000), Jeremy Rifkin (2011), Herman Daly (1996, 2010), and others.

More than merely philosophies of economy, these paradigms represent overlapping features of a complex social and economic transformation of industrial society. The Oxford English Dictionary defines the meaning of the word "paradigm" as "a typical example or pattern of something." Much as Kuhn (1962) used the term "paradigm" to describe preconceptions that situate and condition scientific disciplines, I view the paradigms of KE as contending epistemological frameworks that are competing to displace mass industrial society as a master frame of reference.

Embodying quasi-metaphysical assumptions about the nature and goals of human social development, each paradigm of KE represents a unique conceptualization of the future. Rather than incommensurate ideational systems, I argue that each paradigm of KE is in reality an emerging perspective or feature of a new metaparadigm rooted in a rapidly evolving technological society. While it is true that these discourses have largely subsumed overlapping discussions on social policy, it also the case that these discourses are not all the same.

As Peters (2009b) points out, not all conceptions of KE are simply variations on neoliberal political economy. While some discourses on KE predate neoliberalism, others in fact critique it. Beyond interpretations of KE that reduce its significance to neoliberalism, I consider the long history of shifting notions of KE. In truth, this research is highly critical of the influence of neoliberalism as a policy framework in US social policy. Notwithstanding this criticism, however, the main purpose of this book is to rethink US educational reform in light of emergent changes in economy and society. Moving beyond neoliberal policy constructions of educational reform and building on scholarship in critical educational theory, I am interested to explore new policy frameworks for situating US education in the twenty-first century.

## Research Focus

The importance of education to economic growth has emerged as a common policy framework shaping a wide discourse on educational reform across OECD countries. In fact, it is now commonplace to suggest that education policy has become a subset of economic policy. Neoliberal theories of political economy propose "that human well-being can best be advanced by liberating individual entrepreneurial freedoms and skills within an institutional framework characterized by strong private property rights, free markets, and free trade" (Harvey, 2005, p. 2). Critical scholars, however, argue that these market-driven reforms of social policy reflect "policy ensembles" that are themselves embedded within global economic discourses (Foucault, 1977; Ball, 2006). For this reason, this book is particularly focused on the embedded nature of US education policy.

Building on the work of critical educationalists (e.g., Giroux, 2001, 2003; Apple, 2006; Rizvi and Lingard, 2010; Spring, 2010), I link proposals on educational policy to the need for a new sociopolitical framework that might better situate educational reform. Informed by research data that includes public policy texts on US education produced by the Obama administration, and interviews with scholars and experts whose research and thinking is directly connected to the study of KE and education, this book explores sociopolitical proposals for rethinking US educational reform. I suggest that the concept of KE has subsumed overlapping discussions on the future of advanced economies in the context of ambiguous policy forecasts (Lundvall and Johnson, 1994; OECD, 1996). Drawing from discourses on the Creative Economy, the Network Economy, and the

Green Economy as overlapping hermeneutical systems, I explore policy proposals for transforming US education.

## Document Analysis

Part of the goal of this book is to develop a more nuanced account of KE by examining the many discursive layers that together construct KE as a social imaginary. It is my view, for example, that deconstructing KE is critical both to analyzing the contradictions that structure contemporary discussions on educational reform and improving scholarship on the political economy of education. Research supporting this book utilizes expert interviews and public policy documents in order to generate both a nuanced analysis and a set of recommendations regarding educational policy processes in the United States.

Document review and analysis has been used as a foundation for data collection and the documents used in the study have been selected as key illustrations of the nature and goals of educational reform policy within the Obama administration. These documents include:

1. *A Strategy for American Innovation: Securing Our Economic Growth and Prosperity*, National Economic Council, Council of Economic Advisers, and Office of Science and Technology Policy, 2011.
2. *A Blueprint for Reform: The Reauthorization of the Elementary and Secondary Education Act*, US Department of Education (2010a).
3. *Transforming American Education: Learning Powered by Technology, National Education Technology Plan*, US Department of Education (2010c).

All three documents originate from the first term of the Obama presidency and reflect the key ideas driving President Obama's policy agenda. The selection of documentary evidence outside the domain of education reflects a deliberate attempt to deconstruct the economic theories shaping education policy and examine the thinking supporting these theories.

Documentary evidence is also augmented by research interviews as a means to "triangulate" research data. Together, qualitative interviews and document analyses are viewed as windows into the ongoing construction of KE policies. The use of this research data is understood as a means to deconstruct and evaluate the key economic theories promoting certain kinds of reform in US education. Put differently, my goal in reviewing documentary evidence for this study is to understand the context and conditions shaping the intellectual trends that now drive US educational reform efforts.

## Interview Research

In addition to this documentary evidence, research supporting this book is informed by interviews with scholars and researchers whose expertise overlaps the fields of education, economics, and public policy. My purpose in using these interviews as research data is to better understand and interpret the intellectual strands that now shape conceptualizations of education in a postindustrial society, particularly notions of human capital development. Interview participants have been specifically selected because of their expertise on KE and its relationship to the political economy of education. These experts include:

1. Richard Florida, director of the Martin Prosperity Institute at the University of Toronto and leading proponent on the Creative Economy.
2. Michel Bauwens, founder of the Foundation for Peer-to-Peer Alternatives, and noted expert on the Network Economy.
3. Sam Pitroda, former chairman of India's National Knowledge Commission (2005–2009), advisor to the prime minister of India, and founder and first chairman of India's Telecom Commission.
4. Cathy Davidson, the John Hope Franklin Humanities Institute professor of Interdisciplinary Studies at Duke University, a member of the National Council on the Humanities, and noted expert on digital media and learning.

5. Donald Brinkman, program manager at Microsoft Research in digital humanities, digital heritage, and games for learning, and former program manager with the Education Products Group.
6. Tony Wagner, Innovation Education Fellow at the Technology and Entrepreneurship Center at Harvard University and the founder and codirector of the Change Leadership Group at the Harvard Graduate School of Education.
7. Tony Seba, lecturer on entrepreneurship and clean energy at Stanford University and founder of numerous clean technology companies in Silicon Valley.

The value of using a range of expert interviews to inform research data is that interviewees can offer insight into solutions that lie outside the assumptions of conventional theoretical and methodological frameworks. Indeed, it is often these very assumptions that produce the "problems" under study. By making assumptions explicit, scholars have the means to reexamine the embedded nature of research problems, including hidden motivations and/or deficient reasoning.

## Research Hypothesis

As Hall (1993) suggests, policymaking is a process of social learning. Intended as a contribution to scholarship on the political economy of education, this book seeks to promote an alternative approach to guiding US education policy reform. This includes a particular focus on the genealogy and discourses of KE that now shape forecasts on the future of US society. Drawing insight from discussions on the Creative Economy, the Network Economy, and the Green Economy, I am interested to develop policy proposals for rethinking education policy. Moreover, I wish to build on alternative readings of KE in order to highlight the need for a new policy framework in interpreting and shaping education in the twenty-first century.

My main hypothesis is that educational reform policies are undermined by superficial readings of discourses on KE. Conflating various discourses of KE, educational reform is now rooted in complicated assumptions about the nature and function of education

**Table 0.2** Working premises

1. US education policy is informed by discourses on KE
2. As a policy framework, educational reform policies are undermined by superficial readings of KE
3. Conflating various discursive readings of KE, educational reform is now rooted in contradictory assumptions about the nature and function of education linked to neoliberal interpretations of human capital theory
4. Mapping models or paradigms of KE, scholarship might disentangle these overlapping discourses in order to introduce more effective policy proposals for transforming US education
5. Building on scholarship like this, education policy might begin to consider a new social policy framework that better responds to the challenges confronting postindustrial societies (i.e., technological innovation, labor automation, underemployment, climate change, sustainable innovation, etc.)

within a postindustrial era. Building on the work of Peters (2010), I explore four discrete paradigms of KE and consider their import for shaping a new metaparadigm on educational reform.

Moving beyond neoliberal constructions of education policy, I am interested in developing a new discursive framework for rethinking US educational reform. Building on the work of endogenous growth theory (Romer, 1990), for example, contemporary economic theory explicitly joins investments in education and training to economic development (Becker, 1964, 1975). Recognizing the continued importance of the global economy in shaping education today, I examine the origin of the theories and concepts that shape the notion of KE. Indeed, the orientation of this book is supported by the working premises explained in table 0.2.

## Unpacking Discourses of the Knowledge Economy

The application of research and scholarship to public policy remains an important feature of government policymaking in advanced economies. Neoliberal theorists, for example, maintain that the key to economic growth lies in liberalizing trade, privatizing state assets, and reducing welfare provisions. Over the past three decades, the neoliberal paradigm has emphasized efficiency through the measurement of policy outputs (Clark and Newman, 1997). In education policy, these initiatives include:

> cost recovery and user pays principles; the introduction of school fees even at primary schools; an emphasis on primary education on the assumption that economic returns are greater there than from investment in secondary and tertiary education; putting a budget cap on public funding of education; encouragement of privatization policies and voucher schemes; the introduction of performance management and budgeting schemes; output-based calculations for providing support to education; merit pay for teachers and educational administrators; greater freedom of choice for parents ; standardized tests to facilitate this choice within and across national systems; various other performance contracting schemes; and decentralization of education delivery against a set of nationally agreed upon goal and curriculum expectations. (Rizvi and Lingard, 2010, p. 186)

This research study suggests that there is a need for a new approach to designing social policy in advanced economies. Informed by the work of critical educationalists (e.g., Giroux, 2003; Apple, 2006; Spring, 2008), I approach policy scholarship from within the tradition of critical policy studies, paying particularly close attention to the discourses that now shape the evolution of contemporary educational reform. This involves asking questions with respect to given policies, including context, textual construction, and the means through which educational policies are implemented (Rizvi & Lingard, 2010, p. 52).

Examining the genealogy of KE in the context of forecasts on postindustrial society, I am interested in rethinking the underlying assumptions that anchor US education. While this book critiques the influence of neoliberalism on US social policy, its main goal is to reconsider the purpose and principles of US education in light of diverse readings of KE.

As Peters (2001) suggests, the art of policy scholarship often involves disentangling the discursive threads that combine to influence policy narratives. Despite the fact that KE is most often interpreted as a monolithic discourse, I wish to show that KE is in fact a proliferation of discourses that intersect a wide range of disciplines. Building on this understanding, I map the contours of an expanded model of education policy that is informed by alternative readings of KE. Advancing on theories of the Network Economy, the Creative Economy, and the Green Economy, I consider the potential for a new policy framework for situating educational reform within a broader understanding of KE.

## Structure of this Book

In chapter 1, I attempt to situate education policy in terms of changes in global political economy. As I demonstrate, widespread concern about rejuvenating the US economy overlaps mounting anxiety about a decline in the quality of US education. Correlating national economic challenges with the poor state of US schools, education policy has become increasingly focused on neoliberal social policies. Beyond the era of neoliberalism, I underscore the need to reconsider the value of long-term social investments in the context of national systems of innovation.

In chapter 2, I trace the genealogy of KE as a meta-discourse, looking specifically at the intellectual strands that promote KE as a framework for public policy. I explore the evolution of the concepts and policies that animate the discussion on KE and examine the background literature supporting research for this book. Lastly, I interpret current US education policies in terms of the broader global economic landscape in which these policies are now embedded.

In chapter 3, I trace four contemporary expressions of KE and consider their import for shaping education policy. In addition to neoliberal accounts of KE (Paradigm 1), I examine the Network Economy (Paradigm 2), the Creative Economy (Paradigm 3), and the Green Economy (Paradigm 4). Framing these discourses as paradigms of KE, I seek to demonstrate that contemporary US educational policy misreads both the complexity and ambiguity underlying shifts in the global economic landscape. I outline the book's research focus, including my interest in developing a critical analysis of US education policy. In addition to neoliberal interpretations of KE, I examine variations in the discursive models of

KE with the purpose of better appreciating the need for change in contemporary US education policy. Lastly, I argue that all four paradigms are linked together by a shared emphasis on social and technological transformation.

In chapter 4, I examine public documents produced by the Obama administration. Against a historic background of neoliberal public policies, I argue that recent debates about US education are largely framed by economic discourses linked to globalization and the need for national systems of innovation. This data is viewed as support for interrogating the scope of neoliberal social policies and for rethinking educational reform. My goal in examining these documents is to develop a nuanced scholarship on KE that appreciates the need for multiple readings on educational reform.

In chapter 5, I offer my interpretation of the findings of this research supported by interviews with Richard Florida, Michel Bauwens, Sam Pitroda, Cathy Davidson, Donald Brinkman, Tony Wagner, and Tony Seba. I elaborate on these findings and suggest that educational reform needs to move beyond incremental improvements in transmitting basic academic skills in order to adapt to the needs associated with technological innovation and a global knowledge economy.

In chapter 6, I consider the measures necessary to reshape education policy in postindustrial societies, and offer recommendations for both near- and long-term education in the United States. Informed by the multiple readings of KE, I make conclusions regarding the State structures that now frame contemporary educational policies. Most importantly, I highlight the need for a post-market State framework rooted in theories on social investment and the long-term transformation of a market society.

# Chapter 1

# US Education Policy as Economic Policy

## Human Capital Theory

The idea that education contributes to economic growth is by no means new. The value of skills and knowledge to economic performance was abundantly clear to Adam Smith[1] (1723–1790) as early as the eighteenth century and to William Petty (1623–1687) as early as the seventeenth century. It was not until the 1960s, however, that modern economists began to systematically incorporate the idea of learning and education into economic theory. Evolving out of the work of Mincer (1958), Becker (1964), and Schultz (1961, 1964, 1971), human capital theory (HCT) proposed that capitalist organizations could enhance worker performance and improve productivity by investing in skills and training. Economists began using the metaphor of "capital" (a long-standing concept in economics) to explain the role of education and training in advancing economic performance.

Recent interest among macroeconomists in the potential of learning and education to enhance economic growth builds on theories of endogenous growth, especially *New Growth Theory* (Romer, 1986, 1990). Rather than reducing the value of labor to market transactions, New Growth Theory suggests that increased investments in education have a direct impact on long-run economic expansion. Accordingly, "the stock of human capital determines the rate of growth" (Romer, 1990). Beginning in the mid-1980s, growth theorists began replacing unexplained technical progress (exogenous growth variables) with a model that emphasized investments in human capital as a foundation to economic development. Differing from neoclassical economic theory, growth theorists argue that *endogenous* growth is the outcome of innovation from within an economic system, and not the result of forces that impinge from outside (Romer, 1994, p. 4).

Where neoclassical economic theory focuses on market-based supply and demand, New Growth Theory holds that economic growth rises in proportion to human capital investments. Accordingly, long-run growth depends on policy measures that emphasize investments in education and training.

Given the rising demand for skilled labor, it is hardly surprising that human capital formation has become a widely shared policy goal. Indeed, studies on New Growth Theory overlap an extensive literature on learning management, learning organizations, and skill-biased technological change[2] (Bekman, Bound, & Machin, 1998). Principles underlying human capital formation include techno-scientific innovation, the codification of knowledge through ICTs, the commodification of knowledge through intellectual property regimes, and the production and circulation of knowledge by and through knowledge networks (Peters, 2009b). Notwithstanding the broad consensus on the value of human capital, however, there is significant debate on its definition and scope (Berry & Glaeser, 2005).

Mellander & Florida (2007) point to three widely divergent theories on human capital that problematize any simple definition of the term. As they observe, the first theory of human capital "argues that universities play a key role in creating initial advantages in human capital, which becomes cumulative and self-reinforcing over time." A second theory of human capital "argues that [urban] amenities play a role in attracting and retaining highly-educated, high-skill households" (p. 3). In addition to urban design, a third theory on human capital "argues that tolerance and openness to diversity" facilitate the absorptive capacity for importing the necessary skills for economic expansion.

## Neoliberal Globalization and Educational Reform

Educational reform initiatives are now subsumed by economic policies that emphasize human capital formation over older notions of social development and/or the public good (Rizvi and Lingard, 2010). Where postwar education policy emphasized discourses on national development, education is now more commonly regarded as a feature of discussions on market growth and the "refinement" of human resources. As Garrison (2012, p. 370) observes,

> the marvelous industrial idea of the nineteenth century was the refinement of natural resources into standardized, hence readily interchangeable and replaceable, parts for the national production function. The marvelous postindustrial idea of the twenty-first century is the refinement of human resources into standardized, hence readily interchangeable and replaceable, parts for the global production function. Schools serve as the site for smelting and refining human resources.

This shift in focus reflects a move from the nationalized welfare state of Keynesianism to the global "competition state" of neoliberal globalization (Cerny, 1990). Indeed, it is also paradigmatic of the broad transformation in social policy beginning in the late 1970s. Supported by the economic philosophy of thinkers like Friedrich von Hayek (1944, 1960) and Milton Friedman (1962), social policy has been increasingly shaped by a "negative" theory of the state.

For its advocates, neoliberal social policy reflects an economic philosophy that rejects government intervention in favor of market expansion. For its critics, neoliberal social policy is less grounded in economic philosophy and more ground in a political project: namely, the growing power of transnational corporations and the dilution of the state. To understand the influence of neoliberalism on education over the past three decades, it is important to appreciate the rise of "stagflation" (the simultaneous expansion of unemployment and inflation) in the 1970s.

In answer to the economic crisis of the 1970s, neoliberalism positioned itself as the authority on globalization. Theorists argued that poor government planning and an overly generous welfare state had undermined the organic capacities of self-regulating markets. In response to the "failure" of Keynesian economics, theorists on neoliberalism began promoting policy reforms that simultaneously reduced government intervention while expanding international trade. With the elections of Margaret Thatcher in Britain and Ronald Reagan in the United States, neoliberal policy reforms became the foundation to a new paradigm of government, that many would later describe as the Anglo-Saxon model of political economy (Power, 1996).

Moving policymaking beyond its postwar emphasis on steering markets, neoliberal economists argued that government intervention undermined both productivity and growth through trade. Neoliberal social policies focused on deregulating labor markets, lowering payroll taxes, and reducing labor costs. Where Keynesianism assumed that inflation and recession were mutually exclusive, theories on neoliberalism argued that stagflation and unemployment were due to market distortions.

Persuasive arguments in favor of self-organizing markets proposed that neoliberal globalization was the only solution for resuscitating stagnating economies. Accordingly, social spending and state intervention were in conflict with economic growth. Social expenditures were now viewed as a cost to future economic growth, rather than as a protection against social instability. As a result, Keynesian social policy was downplayed in favor of policies that supported market liberalization.

## The Education Crisis

As Rizvi and Lingard (2010) explain, it is no longer possible to understand education policy within advanced economies without appreciating the central role of neoliberal globalization. Multifaceted policies and programs introduced at the global level have reinforced social policies at the local level geared to stoking human capital performance in the context of increased market competition. Indeed, education is now seen as a vehicle of national competitiveness in which the "global knowledge economy" is a policy axis for coordinating educational reform. Normative discourses on human capital formation are now used to steer the actions and behavior of communities across a wide range of institutions (Lave and Wenger, 1991; Rizvi and Lingard, 2010).

In the United States, economic discourses fixed on the need to introduce new models of education and lifelong learning (LLL)[3] have emphasized science and technology as a means to stimulating future growth. Domestic policy under President Obama has focused on STEM education as a key pillar in rebuilding the US economy:

> With strong educational foundations, Americans will create the leading ideas of the 21st century and ensure that these ideas diffuse throughout the American workforce. On many metrics, however, including grade-level proficiency and college graduation rates, America has slipped behind other countries. We must reform our education and workforce training systems to ensure Americans are qualified for the jobs of tomorrow. This imperative underpins the Obama Administration's focus on education reform in general and in science, technology, engineering, and math (STEM) education in particular. It is also imperative to extend STEM educational and career opportunities to women and minority groups that are underrepresented in these areas, so that all Americans can find quality jobs and lead our innovative economy in the decades ahead. (White House, 2011, p. 15)

Widespread concern about stimulating the US economy for KE overlaps rising anxiety about a decline in the quality of US education. Correlating national economic challenges with the poor state of US schools, education policy has become increasingly focused on tightening standards and enforcing quality control. Much of this anxiety stems from broad changes in the topography of the global economy. Notwithstanding the considerable geopolitical influence of the United States, Europe, and Japan, the social and economic power of China and other newly industrialized economies (NIEs) has grown substantially (Nolan and Pack, 2003).

Growing interest in reforming education for knowledge-based society directly overlaps rising economic challenges faced by OECD countries. Estimates building on the 2008 financial crash, for example, indicate that China could be the largest economy in the world by as early as 2020, and perhaps twice the size of the United States by 2050. Beyond the era of "Western predominance," OECD countries now face increasing pressure to adapt to a very different era in globalization. According to a 2012 forecast by the US National Intelligence Council, "the U.S., European, and Japanese share of global income is projected to fall from 56 percent today to well under half by 2030":

> Asia will have surpassed North America and Europe combined in terms of global power, based upon GDP, population size, military spending, and technological investment. China alone will probably have the largest economy, surpassing that of the United States a few years before 2030. In a tectonic shift, the health of the global economy increasingly will be linked to how well the developing world does—more so than the traditional West. In addition to China, India, and Brazil, regional players such as Colombia, Indonesia, Nigeria, South Africa, and Turkey will become especially important to the global economy. Meanwhile, the economies of Europe, Japan, and Russia are likely to continue their slow relative declines. (National Intelligence Council, 2012, p. iv)

Once the global leader in mass education, secondary school enrollment rates in the United States have been stagnating since the 1970s—even as wage differentials have expanded substantially. As Goldin & Katz (2008) observe,

> educational attainment in the United States was high for most of the twentieth century by the standards of other nations, and the increase in years of education was substantial for most of the century. However, gains in educational attainment in Europe and parts of Asia in the past three decades have been simply staggering. Younger cohorts in these nations have considerably more education than do older cohorts, and many of the younger cohorts have higher education levels than exist in the United States. The US educational system would appear to be flagging not only in terms of quantity but also in terms of quality. (p. 43)

Part of the problem is that the numbers of young adults acquiring advanced education has not increased substantially over the past 30 years (Autor, 2014). However, this can be partly explained by the fact the neoliberal socioeconomic policies in the United States and Britain have stimulated a massive inflation in the costs of higher education.

Public documents over the past three decades, beginning with the seminal *A Nation at Risk: The Imperative for Education Reform*[4]

(National Commission on Excellence in Education, 1983), have become touchstones in the debate on improving educational performance in the United States. As state and federal policymakers have moved to construct multilevel systems of government-driven accountability, high-profile political struggles to shape national curriculum have made testing and accountability the main levers of educational reform (Ravitch, 2011).

In truth, the "education crisis" has been a driving motif for US educational policy for some time. This is despite the fact that there is no obvious correlation between the quality of a country's educational performance and its economic competitiveness (Sahlberg, 2006; Spring, 2008). Extending back through No Child Left Behind Act (2001), the National Commission on Excellence in Education report (1983) and the National Defense Education Act (1958), the primary rationale for the expanded role of federal and state governments in education has been the need to reinvigorate the US economy (McDonnell & Weatherford, 2011).

In the years since the publication of *A Nation as Risk* (ANAR), debates over the form and shape of US educational reform have become highly charged.[5] Critics on the Left contend that ANAR's singular obsession with schools has been used to deflect political attention from policy failures in other domains. The Coleman Report (1966), for example, observed that family background was a far more significant factor in student achievement than school quality. Indeed, a subsequent federally funded report, the Sandia Report (1990), contradicted many of the conclusions of ANAR (indicating, for example, that SAT scores had actually gone up over the latter half of the twentieth century).

Since the 1970s, levels of economic inequality have widened substantially in the United States, and this is closely correlated with a decline in levels of education especially among racial and ethnic minorities. Empirical data comparing OECD countries indicates that market-driven solutions to expanding education—especially higher education—has resulted in marked disparities. As Goldin & Katz (2008) point out:

> institutional factors, to be sure, have played a role in the different inequality experiences among rich nations. Market forces towards increased inequality after 1980 were reinforced in the United States

and the United Kingdom starting under the administrations of President Reagan and Prime Minister Thatcher by the decline of the unions and the erosion of other labor market institutions that once protected low- and middle- income workers. However, the greater growth of wage inequality in the United States has been substantially driven by the slow down in skill-supply growth combined with flexible wage-setting institutions and a less generous social safety net. (p. 329)

## Beyond Schooling as Human Capital Formation

It is now commonplace to suggest that education policy is a subset of economic policy. Critical scholars argue that neoliberal education policies have reduced schooling to a kind of "factory training" in which any ideal of creativity or individuality has been sacrificed to corporate efficiency (Rizvi and Lingard, 2010; Garrison, 2012). While it may be true, for example, that schooling has been tied to economic development since the very formation of common schools in the early nineteenth century (Waks, 2013), it is also case that the broad mission and purpose of public education has shrunk substantially.

Questions about how to improve US education now invariably converge on discussions about standards and assessment, anchored to market-driven pressures to measure and predict human capital performance. Indeed, a proliferation of auditing and evaluation programs have reduced the professional autonomy of teachers, and facilitated an extensive focus on "basic skills" linked to high stakes testing (Means, 2011, p. 220). International performance indicators such as the OECD's Program for International Student Assessment (PISA) have become standard tools for tracking "educational quality" in order to measure, assess, and forecast future economic competitiveness.

In truth, students in the United States have never done particularly well on international tests (Ravitch, 2011). In fact, many scholars now argue that low test scores have had no tangible impact on US economic growth or the country's capacity for innovation. Going back to 1964, for example, the United States placed eleventh out of 12 industrialized countries in the First International Mathematics Study (Waks, 2013). And despite low-quality schools, workforce productivity has increased substantially (Bernstein & Mishel, 2007).[6]

The main criticism is that contemporary education policies are too narrowly focused on accountability frameworks that excessively reduce schooling to worker training (Apple, 2006; McLaren, 2007). The overriding critique is that educational reform does not focus on "educating" citizens but rather on merely training workers. Put differently, many educationalists fear that education has been supplanted by systems of testing and compliance that combine a growing distrust of teachers with a *national testing regime*.

Linked to an unprecedented expansion in charter schooling, for example, the Bush and Obama administrations have concentrated on testing as a foundation to upgrading and standardizing US education (Spring, 2008; Kumashiro, 2012). Darling-Hammond (2010), for example, makes the case that an extreme focus on test scores has resulted in declining competencies in writing, reading, critical thinking, research, and computer skills. More to the point, she argues that the problems with US education are systemic: decades of sanctioning low performance has deceived the public into believing that reform is taking place when in reality inequality has simply expanded.

The United States is not alone in this of course. As education systems have become larger and more complex, many OECD governments have begun looking to market-based solutions to manage demand. This corporatization of education has also meant widespread investments in market-based strategies for achieving accountability and broad-based standardization of curricula. US education policies have become dominated by widespread privatization efforts in the form of voucher initiatives, charter schools, and growing experiments with for-profit secondary education (Saltman, 2003, 2007; Rizvi & Lingard, 2010). Rizvi and Lingard (2010) describe this shift in education policy this way:

> The focus on human capital formation for greater competitiveness has created a demand for more robust regimes of testing. Within nation-states, testing has increasingly reshaped notions of worthwhile knowledge as well as pedagogical practices and has affected teacher professionalism. But beyond testing at the national level, international comparisons have also become important. In policy

terms, comparative performance on testing regimes such as PISA has even become a surrogate measure for determining the quality and effectiveness of national education systems. Indeed, it is no longer possible to understand education policy without an appreciation of the central role that testing and accountability regimes now play in policy development and evaluation. (Rizvi & Lingard, 2010, p. 14)

## Education as Entrepreneurship

A more recent policy response to the need for educational reform has been an argument for tighter coupling between schooling and entrepreneurship (Zhao, 2009, 2012a,b). A 2012 Scandinavian study on improving education across Nordic countries, for example, points to an acute need to develop educational systems that stimulate creativity and innovation. Explicitly critiquing the use of testing to measure learning, it recommends altering established evaluation systems to accommodate entrepreneurial practice in conjunction with national systems of innovation (Chiu, 2012, pp. 49–50). The basic idea here is that formal schooling requires a more vigorous theory on the value of creativity and entrepreneurship in order to ultimately rejuvenate OECD economies.

The overarching argument is that educational systems today remain locked into an outworn factory model of learning that focuses too narrowly on the retention of knowledge over its application. Advocates of entrepreneurial education argue for the need to focus on sustained innovation in the context of knowledge discovery. More than simply developing corporate, "start-ups," this implies joining notions of entrepreneurship to educational programs in order to promote creativity and innovation. In Rae's (2010) terminology, this is "bounded" entrepreneurship. That is, entrepreneurial stewardship that focuses on problem-solving and providing services of wider social value than the market alone can support. He points to four forces driving this change (pp. 592–593):

1. A changing economic and cultural milieu in which social movements now impinge on outmoded economic models.
2. Changing expectations about social responsibility among younger generations facing chronic unemployment.

3. Changes in technological affordances supporting education including personalization, digital media, and practice-based learning.
4. Changes in the financial and economic structure of education.

According to Gibb (2002), education systems need to refocus on the skills and capacities of entrepreneurship linked to theories of social practice (Bourdieu, 1972). From this perspective, the category of entrepreneurship itself is better framed in interdisciplinary terms overlapping embedded social relationships as "communities-of-practice" (Lave & Wenger, 1998). Indeed, Gibb argues that business schools provide an inadequate basis for shaping entrepreneurship education because of a narrow focus on corporatized markets (neoliberalism). Rather than continuing to promote a "dysfuctional ideology of the 'heroic' entrepreneur" (Stronach, 1990; Gibb, 2002, p. 234), he calls for an expanded notion of entrepreneurship that includes microenterprise, nongovernmental organizations (NGOs), public foundations, and community organizations. Gibb (2002) writes:

> Arguably therefore, there is a major need to take entrepreneurship out of the locker room of economics, remove it from the metatheoretical models of Schumpeter *et al.* and place it in a wider interdisciplinary context built upon a more pluralistic and diffused view of society and of the cultural nature of markets. Closer understanding of notions of trust, ethics, morality and values and the way they shape institutions and organizations and lead to informal "ways of doing things" is the key to recognition that needs can be articulated, and supply response developed, without the notion of price being dominant. Moving enterprise and entrepreneurship away from their equivalence with market liberalization (du Gay 2000; Fournier and Grey 1999) allows the entrepreneurial concept to engage more effectively with wider issues of sustainable enterprise development within the context of cultures, social issues and environment. (Gibb, 2002, p. 251)

More than simply *adding* in entrepreneurial training to education, this would mean changing the nature of education itself so that students are increasingly empowered to design and direct their own learning practices. Indeed, building on Gibb (2002), Rae (2010) points to the need for a fundamental break with didactic teaching and learning methods to transform the culture of education as "programmed knowledge" (Christensen, 1997; Christensen, Horn, & Johnson, 2008).

## Conclusion: Paradigm Making and Paradigm Breaking

While it may be true that the industrial model of schooling is now outmoded, it would also seem to be the case that the challenges associated with a postindustrial era are far more substantial than what a market driven model of education alone can solve. Technological innovation and growing technological unemployment suggest the need for a wide array of changes to US education. At the global level, the continued influence of neoliberalism in social policy has made practical revisions to education policy especially difficult. Indeed, the "policy schizophrenia" (Nederveen Pieterse, 2012) that sets economic policy against social policy remains deeply problematic. Nonetheless, it is the case that the history of policymaking reflects changes in paradigm making and paradigm breaking (Polanyi, 1944; Hall, 1993). Periods of deep and sustained policy change are often precipitated by waves of social and economic crisis. In response to the Great Depression and World War II, for example, the era of postwar Keynesianism saw the rise of massive public investments across the United States and Europe (Esping-Andersen, 1990). In the 1980s, Keynesianism was itself supplanted by economic policies based in neoclassical philosophy.

Much as the shift from Keynesianism to neoliberalism demonstrates, structural revolutions in political economy are in fact quite common. Indeed, many now argue that the "Great Recession" has aggravated a wide range of social and economic challenges that require a new policy paradigm. As Hobsbawm (2009) suggests, "Socialism has failed. Now Capitalism is bankrupt. So what comes next?" Calls for austerity measures in Europe and the United States suggest that neoliberal policies remain in favor, but for how long?

Although the history of social and economic policies in the postwar period is generally understood as a story of two waves of state transformation, Hemerijck (2012) argues that theories on social investment represent a third wave of welfare state transformation. Linked to a particular admiration for the social policies of the Nordic welfare state, some analysts suggest that alternatives to neoliberal social policies begin with a renewed focus on education. Beyond neoliberal readings of HCT, there is an escalating interest in recalibrating domestic policies in advanced economies around long-term welfare investments. This includes State-led investments in infrastructure and public goods (Lundvall, 2004; Cimoli, Dosi, & Stiglitz, 2009; Palley, 2011). In fact, new conceptions of State-led socioeconomic investment have been forming as Center-Left counterresponses to laissez-faire public policies since the 1990s (Blair & Shroeder, 1998).

In chapter 2, I examine the origins of the theories and concepts that shape discourses of the knowledge economy. Looking specifically at the intellectual strands that produce these discourses, I consider their influence on contemporary education policy. Additionally, I track recent interest among macroeconomists in the potential of human capital development to stoke economic growth and consider the pervasive influence of neoliberalism on US educational reform.

# Chapter 2

# The Knowledge Economy in Context

## Tracing the Discourses on the Knowledge Economy

When attempting to develop a genealogy of the discourses on knowledge economy (KE), most scholars begin with Peter Drucker's (1969) *The Age of Discontinuity*. However, the truth is that the discourses on KE are interwoven with much older intellectual threads forming across a range of disciplines (Peters, 2001). Shaped by various theories on the evolution of capitalism, KE emerges from a kind of discursive mosaic that is strongly linked to associated notions of "knowledge workers" and "knowledge industries." In fact, the notion of KE reflects a multifaceted set of claims across sociology, economics, and management studies, which suggests that the industrial economy is being transformed by accelerating investments in science, technology, and innovation (Peters, 2009b). Overlapping discussions on the "information age" and the "information society," KE elides with conceptual discussions on postindustrialism and the rising importance of knowledge-based production and consumption.

Tracing the evolution of the concept of KE is challenging because the history of knowledge-based production does not simply begin with the rise of post-Fordism or the notion of postindustrial society. Conventional readings of KE, in fact, coalesce with larger narratives on the evolution of capitalism itself as a system of production (Bell,

1973). Building on Burton-Jones (1999), for example, Kenway et al. (2006) define KE as "knowledge capitalism":

> The knowledge economy is a contemporary and dominant manifestation of capitalism. It is driven by the production, distribution and consumption of knowledge...Apparently, we are all moving inexorably towards an economy, and indeed society, determined and dominated by the following principles: techno-science, techno-scientific innovation, the codification of knowledge through ICTs, the commodification of knowledge through intellectual property regimes, and the production and circulation of knowledge by and through instrumental knowledge workers and networks. (pp. 4–5)

The truth is that the discussion on KE "sits within a complex and interconnected set of discourses that rapidly succeed, replace and overlap one another" (Peters, 2009a, p. 126). This is because divergent and conflicting accounts of KE undermine any monolithic characterization of the term. Intersecting a broad range of theories on the "information economy" (Porat, 1977), the "information revolution" (Lamberton, 1974), and the "information age" (Dizard, 1982), the literature on KE includes a wide number of terms used interchangeably and uncritically by scholars and theorists alike (Peters, 2001).

Even the scholarly literature through which the concept of KE gains currency simply does not consistently locate the origins of the term:

> While it is commonplace to locate the origin of the knowledge/ information economy/society in the work of several key thinkers in the 1960s and to use this as a context for a discussion of current usage, it is less common for scholars to track the intervening development of the concepts. Academic discourses are often de-historicized and the coinage of terms or key influences not contextualized in regard to global or local or counter-discourses. (Kenway et al., 2006, pp. 11–12)

Scholarship on KE begins from a blend of multiple and overlapping discourses (including early economics literature initiated by Friedrich Hayek [1937] and Fritz Machlup [1962]). Indeed, in the social sciences, Bell's (1973) work *The Coming of Post-industrial Society* is a major milestone in the gestation of the scholarship on KE (Beniger, 1986; Dyer-Witheford, 2000). However, Bell himself traces the concept of *knowledge society* to Robert E. Lane's (1966) article, "The Decline of Politics and Ideology in a Knowledgeable Society."

Prior to Bell's work, Machlup (1962) had already begun exploring the economics of knowledge production by subdividing the US economy into knowledge industries (education, research and development, communications media, computers, and information services, including finance, insurance, and real estate). While Kerr (1963) had already begun examining the emergence of the knowledge industry in terms of the changing nature of the university, and the growing concentration of highly educated experts. Moreover, by 1971, Touraine had coined the term "post-industrial society" in his book of the same name.[1]

Indeed, as early as the 1960s, Machlup (1962) was exploring theories of KE with his research on the effects of patents on knowledge industries. In East Asia, Masuda's[2] scholarship had also begun building on the ideas of the "information society" or *johoka shakai* (Masuda, 1968, 1980). Building on this work, Porat (1977) explored economic measures for an information economy, distinguishing between primary and secondary information sectors. While within the sphere of management studies, Drucker's (1969) exposition on the rise of knowledge workers became a touchstone for many public policy conceptions of KE. His adoption and reworking of Machlup's research served to anchor public policy themes on KE to notions of a coming power shift—from the owners and managers of capital to white-collar workers and specialists.

Ultimately, it would be Bell's (1973) focus on the complex transformation of industrial economy, however, that would come to shape much of the discourse on KE. For Bell, postindustrial society corresponded to new structures of economy and society in which information displaced energy, ICTs displaced machine technologies, and skilled labor displaced semi-skilled labor.

## The Knowledge Economy as Policy Discourse

A common concern with the scholarship on KE is a general lack of analytical rigor. KE policy, for example, reflects policymaking as *futurology* in which the "knowledge economy" often functions as a kind of cultural trope for promoting certain sets of policies (Peters, 2001). In truth, KE discourse has largely become a kind of policy language-game:

> The rules of this policy language-game seem based upon the invention of new metanarratives—overarching concepts or visions of the future—as a method of picturing these changes and presenting a coherent policy narrative. Thus, the terms "postindustrial society," "information society" (which have been around since the late 1960s) and "global information economy" abound in policy documents. More recently, the terms "knowledge" and "learning"—conceptualised both in relation to "society" and economy—have come to occupy centre stage in national policy documents concerned with mapping the impact of global trends and encouraging greater competitiveness and more synergistic relationships between education and the economy. (Peters, 2001, p. 4)

As Peters suggests, KE policies are steeped in hyperbole that is inflated by economic forecasts without regard for historical analysis or interpretation (Peters, 2001, p. 12). In fact, these discourses have been at the root of four decades of "deindustrialization" in the United States and other advanced economies. In fact, as I examine below, the recent collapse of "financialization"—as the antidote to deindustrialization—has bolstered support for greater industrial intervention and major new political shifts in US economic policy.

Close to two decades since the OECD publication of *The Knowledge-Based Economy* (1996), the term "knowledge economy" has largely subsumed older and related conceptions, including the information society/economy, network society, and learning economy. As Nederveen Pieterse (2010, p. 404) notes,

> these ideas are extensions of the idea of postindustrial society, Toffler's "third wave" and the knowledge economy. Technological transformation is widely viewed as a major driver of economic change; in Schumpeterian perspectives, innovation is viewed as key to the business cycle and to the fifty-year long wave or Kondratieff cycle. Thus, science and technology policies are central to economic policy. Universities play a strategic role in knowledge and science and technology upgrading. Research parks and partnerships

between universities and corporations embody this approach. Patent and licensing lawyers are to convert innovations into intellectual property...

Taken literally the concept of the knowledge economy denotes an economy and society "organized around the production of knowledge in the same sense that an agrarian society is organized around agricultural production and an industrial society is organized around manufacture" (Bereiter, 2002, p. 2). Put differently, the common view today is that a knowledge-based society refers to a society dependent on knowledge discovery to drive innovation.

At the global level, KE policy discourse is now rooted in major reports like *The Knowledge-Based Economy* (1996) as a formal policy driver of the "knowledge-based society." Divided into three sections, the report outlines the trends and implications of KE, the role of the science system to national systems of innovation (NSI), and the growing need for economic indicators (Foray, 2004). Perhaps, most importantly, the OECD report categorizes the main features of KE, including knowledge distribution networks (formal and informal), the need for highly skilled labor (human capital), the importance of ICTs, the globalization of labor and economic activity, and the need for government leadership in scientific research and development (R&D).

A powerful driver of public policy across supranational bodies, many of the discourses on KE have focused attention on issues of intellectual property (IP) and the global regulation of creativity and innovation through organizations like the World Intellectual Property Organization (WIPO) and the World Trade Organization (WTO). In this way, IP rights (copyrights, patents, and trademarks) are viewed as fundamental to protecting "knowledge-based capital" (KBC). While knowledge may be abundant, what is scarce is the capacity to apply knowledge to fuel innovation. As Powell and Snellman (2004) observe, this reflects an increasing relative share of GDP attributable to "intangible" capital. This also includes "a greater reliance on intellectual capabilities [over] physical inputs or natural resources" and a deliberate effort "to integrate improvements in every stage of the production process, from the R&D lab to the factory floor to the interface with customers" (Powell & Snellman, 2004, p. 201).

## Globalization and the Knowledge Economy

Confronting economic stagnation, governments across many OECD countries have begun constructing industrial policies built on top of theories of entrepreneurial innovation. Moving past debates around "strategic industries" (such as semiconductors or advanced manufacturing), US public policy under the Obama administration has refocused on innovation policy in response to the broad sweep of challenges facing the United States (Pages, 2010). Indeed, according to Goldman Sachs, the US share of global GDP fell from 31 percent in 2000 to 27.7 percent in 2006, even as the share for BRIC countries rose to 11 percent from 7.8 percent (Gross, 2007). Even adjusting for the differential power of currencies, growth in the United States has lagged behind global growth for the past ten years.[3]

Although it may be true that the contemporary global economic map is the outcome of a long evolution in the relationship between the structures and flows of goods, peoples, and ideas (path dependence), it is also the case that old geographies of production, distribution, and consumption are now being eclipsed by the rise of new geographies. Indeed, the growing economic power of many developing economies has been striking. Data over the past two decades indicates that developing countries are now seeing a substantial increase in their share of economic power, particularly in terms of their share of global GDP, their share of exports, and their share of inward flows of foreign direct investment (Dicken, 2011, p. 25).

Beyond advanced economies, globalization has begun changing the topography of mass manufacturing, moving the locus of economic power "Eastward." Asia's stock markets now account for 32 percent of global market capitalization (ahead of the United States at 30% and Europe at 25%) (Zoellick, 2010), with China alone accounting for 5.4 percent. As Dicken (2011, p. 525) observes,

> Without doubt, the biggest single global shift reshaping the contours of the global economic map is the resurgence of East Asia to a position of global significance, commensurate with its importance before "the West" overtook it in the nineteenth century. But this has not been a sudden event. Like the tectonic processes that reshape the earth's crust, the build-up takes time before we become aware of the

true magnitude of the change... The result is a shift in the center of gravity of the world economy, a shift that seems now to be on solid foundations and not a mere passing phase.

This tectonic shift is marked by a perceptible decline in confidence across many developed countries particularly in the United States (Beattie, 2005; Nederveen Pieterse, 2011; Araya and Marber, 2013). Indeed, economic policy in many OECD countries is now increasingly marked by a growing fear of economic decline.[4] This fear has been exacerbated by the expanding geopolitical influence of China and the other BRICs (Brazil, Russia, India, China).[5] What is obvious is that the rise of NIEs now poses a direct challenge to rudimentary notions of KE developed over the past half century (Fukuyama, 2012).

As NIEs have become increasingly stronger in industrial manufacturing, advanced economies have been forced to maintain permanent cycles of innovation to *stay ahead* (Christensen, 1997; Freeman and Soete, 1997; Foster & Kaplan, 2002). This is particularly true in the United States. The Obama administration has applied significant political capital in promoting broad investments in frontier technologies including nanotechnology, biotechnology, additive manufacturing (3D Printing), and robotics.

## Beyond Neoliberalism

Change in the structure of globalization has challenged leaders in many developed economies to refocus on advanced manufacturing and human capital development as key instruments in rejuvenating stalled economies. In truth, educational reform is now part of a titanic struggle to rejuvenate OECD economies even as Fordist mass production systems have been displaced to low-cost zones in developing countries. As deindustrialization has taken root in many advanced economies, economic stagnation has been increasingly explained in terms of a decline in productivity and/or increased global competition.

Indeed, for the first time since the Great Depression, job growth over the past decade has been anemic. Growing underemployment appears to reflect deep structural issues that will likely worsen.

Brynjolfsson and McAfee (2014, p. 36), for example, point to the fact that the Bureau of Labor Statistics' Job Opening and Labor Turnover Survey (JOLTS) reveals a dramatic decrease in hiring since 2000. Approximately 12 million jobs were lost in the United States between 2007 and 2009 with the unemployment rate reaching close to 10 percent of the US workforce. While the unemployment rate has come down significantly since its high in 2009, there remains significant trepidation about the future of labor across advanced economies.

Increased economic output has historically meant increased employment but this no longer appears to be the case. In many advanced economies, unemployment now remains at record levels and financial fragility has become the norm. Brynjolfsson & McAfee (2011) note that there are three leading theories for explaining this high unemployment: the first, linked to economic theories on economic cyclicality; the second, linked to theories of technological stagnation; and the third, linked to theories of computer automation:

1. The cyclical explanation suggests that deep recessions are followed by slow cyclical recoveries. Jobs are lost but eventually regained as markets move to correct themselves (Florida, 2011).
2. The stagnation explanation suggests that advanced economies have in fact reached a "technological plateau." Innovation has slowed or generally been less transformational on the economy generating fewer new jobs (Cowen, 2011).
3. The automation explanation suggests that mounting technological innovation is not slowing but expanding considerably and building on computation to automate various forms of labor. Accordingly, labor will continue to be displaced at an accelerating rate (Rifkin, 2011).

In fact, according to a recent study (Godofsky, Zukin, & Horn, 2011), only 53 percent of US college students graduating between 2006 and 2010 now hold full-time jobs. Outside the United States, growing technological productivity and population growth are producing a global jobs crisis, especially for young people. As Zhao (2012b) observes,

> the dire unemployment situation for youth has reached a crisis level, not only in the U.S., but globally. In July 2011, there were over four

million unemployed youth in the United States, meaning that more than 18% of the 16- to 24-year old Americans were unemployed (Bureau of Labor Statistics, 2011). In the United Kingdom, over one million youth did not have a job in 2011 (Allen, 2011). The situation in other European countries is worse... The average unemployment rate in OECD... member countries, 34 of the richest nations on Earth, was over 16% in 2010 (OECD, 2011) and was expected to reach 18% in 2011 (OECD, 2010). (p. 51)

Despite the fact that policymakers in OECD countries largely agree on the need for educational reform in support of workforce development and LLL, the substance of that reform remains poorly defined. The basic assumption governing education today is that schools must generate better human capital. Coupled to an instrumentalist rationale, the discourse on education as human capital development is itself supported by a neoliberal social imaginary that builds on market facing public policies (Rizvi & Lingard, 2010).

Over the past three decades neoliberal social policies have shaped global trends on education policy. Part of the challenge facing neoliberal interpretations of social policy, however, is an ostensive indifference toward widening inequality and deepening structural unemployment. Indeed, over the past decade, a growing number of intergovernmental organizations (IGOs) have promoted alternative policy models challenging neoliberal social policies. Policy proposals have included UNICEF's (2000) report on rising childhood poverty and the OECD's *Starting strong* (2006), *Understanding the social outcomes of learning* (2007b), and *Growing unequal* (2008a).

Many optimists suggest that we are in the early stages of a "post-neoliberal era." What we do know is that social inequality in the United States now mirrors that of the Great Depression (Piketty & Saez, 2012). In fact, median incomes have been stagnating in real terms since the 1970s. In 1974, for example, the top 1 percent of families consumed 9 percent of US GDP. By 2007, that share had increased to 23.5 percent. In fact, since 2002 a mere 1 percent of US households have consumed 65 percent of all the growth in the economy. To put this in perspective, consider the fact that between 1995 and 2007 the top 0.01 percent of US households (14,588 families with incomes above $11,477,000) doubled their share of the national income, from 3 percent to 6 percent (Brynjolfsson & McAfee, 2011).

## The US National Innovation System

Over the past three decades, liberalizing trade and investment policies have introduced a growing density of trade in goods, capital, and ideas. Today, nearly one quarter of the $70 trillion dollar global economy results from international trade. As Marber (2014) observes,

> Over the last generation or two, the world has been transformed into a complex system of interdependent and constantly changing relationships. No longer a patchwork quilt, the global economy today is an interwoven tapestry. Global production and distribution chains mesh Brazilian iron mines, Greek ships, Chinese steelmakers, German automakers, Wall Street banks, and car dealers in Peoria. Financial markets instantly entangle California pension funds, insurers in Asia, and Cayman Island hedge funds with banks everywhere.

Since the 2008 financial crash, however, neoliberal constructions of US economic and social policy have become increasingly untenable. Indeed, real incomes in the United States have declined significantly over the last three decades even as income inequality has swelled. A decline in the social fabric supporting US society has moved many scholars to openly worry about a rising "economic feudalism" undermining the social stability of the country (Saltman, 2010b; Freeman, 2012; Piketty, 2014).

Deterioration in the Gini coefficient (the statistical measure of income equality) indicates that inequality in the US labor force has risen substantially (Marber, 2014). This growing inequality is also tied to education. In the United States, school quality is determined by property taxes and thus real estate value. Wealthier neighborhoods necessarily spend more on education than poorer neighborhoods. Within this funding structure, good schools get better over time while bad schools often get worse. Darling-Hammond (2010), for example, makes the case that systemic underfunding has encouraged a sharp national divide in the US labor force. Pointing to the poor state of many US schools, she chronicles the mismatch between the US education system and the changing demands of a global knowledge economy. Part of the problem is that high-performing countries such as Singapore, Finland, and South Korea largely draw teachers from the top-third of the academic pool, while in the United States it is most often the bottom-third (*Economist*, 2013b).

The truth is that there is more to the United States than neoliberalism. Despite the fact that contemporary theories on the "varieties of capitalism" (Hall and Soskice, 2001) tend to reduce the United States to a prototypical neoliberal economy, it would be wrong to conclude that the United States lacks a history of state intervention. Indeed, a closer analysis of US policy reveals historical variations in the relative importance of market forces over the course of the country's history (Bauer, 2012). Notwithstanding a strong philosophical belief in markets, government has played a key role in US economic strategy over the course of the country's history. As Bauer (2012, p. 105) points out, this "role has changed over time, but it continues to be multi-faceted and distributed. It is this differentiated, parallel and sometimes redundant nature of efforts that has historically fuelled the dynamism of the U.S. innovation system."

US public policy has been deeply invested in stoking new technologies across various industries. Early investments in radar, satellite and GPS, computing, digital imaging, and the Internet, for example, have shaped whole fields of research. Indeed, Block and Keller (2011) point to specific and discrete phases in the US *national innovation system* (NIS) in shaping the US economy. These developmental phases have included World War II, the Cold War, and, most recently, the era of Neoliberalism.

In what might be described as the fourth phase of the US innovation system, the Obama administration has made a concerted effort to reconstruct national innovation policy (Pages, 2010). In conjunction with a broad shift toward neo-Keynesian policy reforms, education policy has now become explicitly coordinated with policies designed to reinforce the building blocks of US innovation strategy.[6] With the goal of "out-innovating, out-building, out-competing, and out-educating" the rest of the world, President Obama has promoted a wide range of initiatives in clean energy, biotechnology, nanotechnology, and space application in an effort to steer US policymaking beyond the era of neoliberalism. Policy and planning outlined in *A Strategy for American Innovation: Securing Our Economic Growth and Prosperity* (White House, 2011) reflect an intensive effort to redesign NIS policy:

> By championing policies that facilitate marketplace innovation, the federal government will continue to be an essential partner in the U.S. national innovation system. To that end, the Obama administration

will take appropriate public action by supporting an environment in which innovation is rewarded and best practices are diffused, investing in a technically capable workforce, supporting basic scientific discoveries, and promoting the development of the technology platforms from which future innovations will spring. Government direction can never be a substitute for the free market conditions that propel American innovation. But government must act to support those conditions and ensure that innovation, the engine of our prosperity, drives America further and faster towards higher quality jobs, healthier and longer lives, new opportunities and new industries, and the ever-expanding technological frontier. (p. 13)

Responding to fears of US economic decline, the Obama administration has deployed substantial funding for strategic investments in renewable energy, energy efficiency, and information technologies, including tens of billions of dollars in research and development (R&D). This includes sizable investments in a new publicly funded research agency focused on clean energy known as ARPA-E (Advanced Research Projects Agency Energy),[7] modeled on DARPA (Defense Advanced Research Projects Agency).

In fact, a key theme of the American Recovery and Reinvestment Act (ARRA) has been a focus on the Green Economy. This includes the allocation of significant funds to the Department of Energy in a bid to move the United States beyond fossil fuels. This also includes hundreds of millions of dollars allocated to firms (through matching funds and loan programs) to support the development of solar panels, electric batteries, biofuels, and other green technologies. Indeed, in 2009 the Department of Energy (DOE) "was awarded $377 million in funding for 46 new multi-million dollar energy frontier research centers (EFRCs) located at universities, national laboratories, nonprofit organisations, and private firms throughout the U.S." (Mazzucato, 2011, p. 105).

Even prior to the Obama administration, the Bush administration had championed a substantial innovation strategy of its own. The 2007 America COMPETES[8] Act, for example, provisioned a wide range of funding initiatives designed to bolster the "international competitiveness of the United States." Reauthorized in 2010 and signed into law by President Obama in 2011, America COMPETES pays considerable attention to educating future STEM professionals, including increased funding for STEM fields.

## The NIS State

Notwithstanding the fact that state intervention has been key to US innovation throughout its history, its policy importance has grown substantially since the 2008 economic crisis. Beyond the era of neoliberalism, the Obama administration has focused on NIS strategy as a key feature of what some analysts now describe as the era of "gated globalization" (*Economist*, 2013). Indeed, as Dicken (2011) notes, NIS strategy has been a policy foundation of OECD countries "ever since Britain emerged as the world's first fully industrialized nation in the late eighteenth and early nineteenth centuries" (p. 190). The truth is that industrializing countries have used innovation policy to build competitive industries for over a century. One of the world's poorest countries a generation ago, China has leveraged State investments to build an economy that may soon eclipse that of the United States. Scholars may argue about the reasons for China's rapid development, but the fact is that government-driven public investment has been central to China's dramatic economic transformation (Araya, 2013).

The term "national innovation system" (table 2.1) was actually first coined by Bengt-Åke Lundvall (1992) to refer to the network of

**Table 2.1** Definitions of NIS

- The network of institutions in the public and private sectors whose activities and interactions initiate, import, modify and diffuse new technologies (Freeman, 1987).
- The elements and relationships which interact in the production, diffusion and use of new, and economically useful, knowledge... and are either located within or rooted inside the borders of a nation state (Lundvall, 1992).
- A set of institutions whose interactions determine the innovative performance... of national firms (Nelson, 1993).
- The national institutions, their incentive structures and their competencies that determine the rate and direction of technological learning (or the volume and composition of change generating activities) in a country (Patel and Pavitt, 1994).
- That set of distinct institutions that jointly and individually contribute to the development and diffusion of new technologies and which provide the framework within which governments form and implement policies to influence the innovation process. As such, it is a system of interconnected institutions to create, store, and transfer the knowledge, skills, and artifacts that define new technologies (Metcalfe, 1995).

*Source*: Based on OECD (1997)

institutions that jointly facilitate the creation, transfer, and diffusion of new knowledge, skills, and practices (Metcalfe, 1995). According to NIS theory, government-driven innovation policy is critical to promoting collaboration *across* institutional networks:

> The national innovation systems approach stresses that the flows of technology and information among people, enterprises and institutions are key to the innovative process. Innovation and technology development are the result of a complex set of relationships among actors in the system, which includes enterprises, universities and government research institutes. For policy-makers, an understanding of the national innovation system can help identify leverage points for enhancing innovative performance and overall competitiveness. It can assist in pinpointing mismatches within the system, both among institutions and in relation to government policies, which can thwart technology development and innovation. Policies which seek to improve networking among the actors and institutions in the system and which aim at enhancing the innovative capacity of firms, particularly their ability to identify and absorb technologies, are most valuable in this context. (OECD, 1997, p. 7)

Based on the ideas of the nineteenth-century German economist Friedrich List, NIS theory builds on List's (1909) studies of "National System of Political Economy," particularly German industrialization vis-à-vis England. Rooted in List's work, Lundvall (1992) and Freeman (1987) applied NIS theory to interpreting postwar industrialization in Europe and Asia. Pointing to List's emphasis on "endogenous growth" and particularly investments in new technologies, Freeman's research drew heavily on NIS theory to account for the dramatic rise of Japan as a global economic superpower.

In the current environment, NIS theory reflects the increasing attention given to the economic role of knowledge, particularly investments in R&D, education and training, and "codified" knowledge (publications, patents, and other sources). This builds on Freeman's (1987) work linking endogenous growth theory (EGT) to Schumpeter's (1976 [1942]) ideas on entrepreneurship.[9] Today, Schumpeter's (1976 [1942]) thinking on entrepreneurial innovation—together with Porter's (1990) theories on industrial clusters—have become the basis for innovation policy across OECD countries.

## Return of the State

Perhaps the key challenge facing the United States today is the need to reexamine the role of the State itself. In response to the increasing structural problems overlapping child poverty, economic stratification, unemployment, and environmental deterioration, the United States is now challenged to move beyond neoliberalism as a national policy framework. The reason for this is obvious. At its base, neoliberalism supports a negative theory of the state but in the context of KE, neoliberal social and economic policies are clearly outmoded (Lundvall, 2004).

One of the many consequences of the 2008 financial crisis is that the US economic system has been seen as having failed. After decades of the Washington Consensus,[10] even young economists at the World Bank appear to be moving toward Asian-styled industrial policies (see Lin & Chang, 2009; Lin & Monga, 2011). As Rae (2010) notes, a rising uncertainty about the future prosperity of advanced economies has produced a backlash against laissez-faire policies altogether:

> The crisis of 2008 is markedly different from the cyclical recessions of the early 1980s and 1990s, which were followed by sustained economic growth. For whilst a gradual cyclical recovery is occurring, underlying economic fundamentals have changed permanently in the USA and UK. The relationships between banks, government, businesses and consumers have changed, with a long-term loss of confidence in the banking and financial services industry. Public debt and its financing costs will remain at high levels for a long period. Western economies are in long-term economic decline in comparison with the growth economies of South East Asia. Public services, especially higher education, are experiencing significant reductions in State funding, and commitments such as guaranteed public pensions are increasingly unaffordable. (p. 595)

Kenway et al. (2006), for example, note the "problem of stimulus." Neoclassical interpretations of KE rest on the assumption that commodity exchange "as a motivation for the exchange and circulation of knowledge" stokes innovation (p. 54). But as Rae (2010) points out, the growing importance of entrepreneurial clusters that speed up the rate of innovation (Schumpeter's "creative destruction") are a much better guage for changes in postindustrial society than market-based commodity exchange. Indeed, the historic strength of the US model has been its capacity to actively create markets for new technologies through government-driven social and financial investments.

The reality is that the economics of innovation are not well understood. As Mazzucato (2011) points out, the single greatest feature of the US innovation system has been its liberal use of State institutions such as the Defense Advanced Research Projects Agency (DARPA), the National Aeronautical Space Agency (NASA), the National Science Foundation (NSF), and the Small Business Innovation Research Program (SBIR) in order to incubate and grow the country's entrepreneurial capacity. As she elaborates, government has "been more about fixing 'network failures' than about 'market failure.'... government's willingness to think big and take risks has created new opportunities and markets, whereas the private sector has shied away because of the long time horizons and the high failure rates" (p. 91).

Presenting a broad critique of the assumptions undergirding neoliberal economic policy, Mazzucato (2011) deconstructs the myths that have shaped Anglo-American views on the State. Noting the historical role of government in steering the US innovation system, she points to federal investments that continue to underwrite large swathes of the US economy. This includes historic investments in early-stage technologies such as jet aircraft, nuclear energy, computing, Internet technologies, lasers, and biotechnology, and more recent investments in energy, technology, and aerospace. This also includes upward of $700 billion (4.5% of GDP) spent annually (fiscal year 2012) on the world's largest military (or 43% of the world's total spending).

As Mazzucato observes, part of the value of government-led investments has been the capacity of the government to catalyze long-run growth cycles. In addition to supporting basic science, government remains critical to mobilizing ideas and resources, and promoting lateral collaboration across institutions. In the pharmaceutical sector, for example, innovation can take up to 17 years "from the beginning of an R&D project to the end" costing as much as $403 million per drug with "only 1 in 10,000 compounds reach[ing] market approval phase, a success rate of 0.01 per cent" (Mazzucato, 2011, p. 50).

## Toward the Social Investment State

Where neoliberal theories on KE emphasize the importance of private investments in R&D, Lundvall and Lorenz (2012) and other NIS theorists emphasize social investment aligned to the needs of rethinking socioeconomic development. Emerging from think tanks and ad hoc policymaking and diffused through the 2000 Lisbon Agenda, *Social Investment Theory* has been positioned as a counter model to neoliberalism (Jenson & Saint-Martin, 2003). Theorists on social investment policy argue that national and/or regional economic strategies need to be more clearly focused on long-term investments that promote skilled autonomy and creative practice (Lundvall & Lorenz, 2012). Accordingly, the key to the future prosperity of advanced economies is a strategic transition of national labor systems into sectors that are "less exposed to global competition" (Lundvall & Lorenz, 2012, p. 237).

Indeed, the value of NIS strategy in understanding the changing political economy of education today is that it offers a framework for interpreting changes in the trajectory of US policymaking. As Marber (2014) observes, standard growth theories suggest that countries that continuously invest in infrastructure and capital goods tend to outgrow those that simply rely on consumer spending. This is not to say that NIS strategy is monolithic. Outside the United States, for example, innovation strategy has been applied through a variety of policy instruments across a range of industries. In the EU, innovation policies are often linked to *social market capitalism*. In France, NIS policies promote public ownership over lucrative state enterprises, while in Germany NIS policies balance innovation and an advanced manufacturing base with state investments supporting competitive domestic firms (Dicken, 2011).

Building on NIS strategy, what is new in Social Investment Theory is a timely focus on social goods as necessary long-term investments. Indeed, the strength of Social Investment Theory is its emphasis on human capacitation and labor force participation as key reforms to the Keynesian welfare state (Lundvall & Johnson, 1994; Lundvall, 2004). Overlapping theories on endogenous growth, Social Investment Theory bridges the economic need for human capital with the political and social need for expanding economic opportunity in the context of globalization. Put differently, alongside its market focus, social investment policy opens space for new discussions on pragmatic welfare policies that can respond to emergent socioeconomic challenges.

The concept of the social investment state argues for the need to redesign social policy in response to the increasing pace of knowledge obsolescence. Underlying the social investment literature is a stress on active welfare policies that respond to growing social challenges facing postindustrial societies (OECD, 2006). Advancing on emergent social challenges overlapping gender equality, skills atrophy, aging demographics, immigration reform, and LLL (Esping-Andersen, Gallie, Hemerijck, & Myles, 2002), the social investment perspective rests on three principles (Jenson, 2010, p. 61):

1. Learning as the pillar of economies and societies of the future with significant policy attention to human capital, beginning with preschool children.
2. Future-oriented policy that ameliorates conditions in the here and now through promotion of social spending designed to break the intergenerational cycle of poverty with a specific focus on children.
3. Investment in community as a whole linked to child-centered policy interventions.

Primarily concerned with economic sustainability, social investment policy narrows the expectations of the welfare state to focus on the relationship between the productive capacities of the active population vis-à-vis the needs of the inactive population. Uniquely, this expansion of public services is focused on supporting female labor force participation through changes to welfare provisions including quality childcare.

Hemerijck (2012) suggests that the Social Investment Theory is rooted in the Nordic "social democratic" model particularly the Swedish welfare state of the 1930s. Building on the social policies of Alva and Gunnar Myrdal (1934), State-led support for education and health care is seen as a long-term investment in the future prosperity of postindustrial societies. From this perspective, the focus is on targeted provisions for the young and on their future employment (Jenson and Saint-Martin, 2003) with the belief that "solid investments in children now will diminish welfare problems among future adults" (Esping-Andersen et al., 2002, p. 51). Where neoliberal theorists underscore the value of self-regulating markets, social investment theorists point to the long-term importance of articulated investments in education and social welfare.

In the United Kingdom (UK), Social Investment Theory is linked to Third Way politics and Tony Blair's New Labour Government (Giddens, 1998). Moving beyond "passive" income compensation and toward "active" citizenship, Third Way social investment frames changes to the welfare state in terms of human capital development and enhanced labor market participation (Perkins, Nelms, & Smyth 2004). Where the old welfare state sought to protect people from the market, the Third Way model of social investment focuses on "tying rights to responsibilities" (Giddens, 1998). From this perspective, public investment imposes responsibilities on individuals and society to transform and enhance economic competitiveness (Lister, 2003, p. 437). Beyond redistributive or consumption-based social welfare (centered on benefits and rights), Giddens (1998) frames social investment in terms of *positive* welfare and a citizenry of "responsible risk takers."

Social Investment Theory is not limited to the UK, however. In fact, many social investment scholars criticize Giddens's approach on the basis of the need for *both* social promotion and social protection (Dobrowolsky, 2002; Lister, 2003; Featherstone, 2006; Jenson, 2010). Scholars searching for policies to supersede neoliberalism have focused on emphasizing policy measures that mitigate against mass unemployment/ underemployment, particularly through education (OECD, 1996; OECD, 2006). This is partly explained in terms of the need for new social policies linked to postindustrialization. In the context of NIS strategy, for example, Lundvall and Lorenz (2012) emphasize national systems of learning that promote *flexicurity* in welfare provisions in support of human capital development.[11]

## Conclusion

Taken as a whole, the literature on social investment deliberately attempts to legitimize government steering through social policy. This includes a counter response to the rise of competition from emerging economies and a recognition of the changing demographic structure of labor markets in OECD countries (Taylor-Gooby, 2004). In administrative terms, this means deploying policies that "prepare" individuals, families, and societies to adapt to changing career patterns and new social configurations in a global knowledge economy (Hemerijck, 2011, p. 12).

In the next chapter, I explore the evolution of the concepts and policies that together form the paradigms of KE, and review the background literature supporting this book. I examine these paradigms of KE in detail with the goal of better understanding the significance of each for shaping new models of US education policy. Taken together, the Neoliberal Knowledge Economy, the Creative Economy, the Network Economy, and the Green Economy reflect contingent yet contradictory intellectual discourses that promote divergent forecasts on postindustrial society. At the same time, each paradigm builds on a common cultural narrative of social transformation that continues to shape policymaking forecasts in advanced economies.

# Chapter 3

# Paradigms of the Knowledge Economy

Contemporary US educational policy reflects a particular set of discourses that elide with forecasts on a global knowledge economy. Tensions between various readings of KE, however, suggest that these discourses are not monolithic. Employing different methodologies and reaching different and sometimes contradictory conclusions, discourses on KE overlap a broad range of fields and disciplines in the production and consumption of policymaking. Indeed, Peters (2009b, pp. 2–3) lists some 20 separate discursive strands on KE overlapping sociology, philosophy, and economics that inform multiple readings of postindustrial society (table 3.1).

In this chapter, I explore the evolution of the concepts and theories that drive the discourses on KE and examine their supporting literature. Analyzing the features of these discourses, I am interested in their import for shaping US education policy. In addition to neoliberal readings of KE (Paradigm 1) outlined in chapter 2, I examine the Network Economy (Paradigm 2), the Creative Economy (Paradigm 3), and the Green Economy (Paradigm 4). Tracing the social contours of these paradigms of KE, I consider their relative similarities and differences (see table 3.1) and argue that contemporary US educational policy misreads both their complexity and ambiguity. I argue that each model or paradigm seeks to broadly define KE by highlighting a particular feature of ongoing mutations in capitalist economy (table 3.2).

**Table 3.1** Multiple discourses on the Knowledge Economy

- Studies on the economic value of knowledge by Fritz Machlup (1962), examining the production and distribution of knowledge in the United States
- Gary Becker's (1964, 1975) analysis of human capital with reference to education
- Peter Drucker's (1969) emphasis on "knowledge workers," coining the term in 1959 and founding "knowledge management"
- Daniel Bell's (1973) sociology of postindustrialism, emphasizing the centrality of theoretical knowledge and the new science-based industries
- Alan Touraine's (1971) *The post-industrial society*, hypothesizing a "programmed society" run by a "technocracy" who control information and communication
- Mark Granovetter's (1973) theorizing of the role of information in the market based on weak ties and social networks
- Mark Porat's (1977) definition of "the information society" for the US Department of Commerce
- Alvin Toffler's (1980) analysis of knowledge-based production in the "Third Wave" economy
- Jean-Francois Lyotard's (1984) theories on "The postmodern condition," as an age marked by the incredulity toward metanarratives"
- James Coleman's analysis of how social capital creates human capital and the development and application of related notions by Pierre Bourdieu (1986) and Robert Putnam (2000)
- The standard or received business model associated with knowledge management prevalent in the 1980s and becoming an established disciple in 1991 (Nonaka, 1991)
- Paul Romer's (1990) argument that growth is driven by technological change arising from intentional investment decisions where technology as an input is a nonrival, partially excludable good
- The "new economy" reading of the decades of the 1990s (Delong 1998; Stiglitz, 1999)
- The OECD's (1996) influential model based on endogenous growth theory and its use of the term "knowledge-based economy"
- Joseph Stiglitz's (1999) emphasis on the World Bank's Knowledge for Development and Education for the Knowledge Economy based on knowledge as a public good
- "The learning economy" developed by Lundvall (1994, with Johnson; 2006, with Lorenz)
- The digital or "weightless" economy proposed by Danny Quah (2003) and others
- The "global information society" based on the World Summit on the Information Society (WSIS)
- Postmodern global systems theory based on network theory, after Manuel Castells (1946, 2000)
- Public policy applications and developments of the "knowledge economy" concept (Rooney et al., 2003; Hearn & Rooney, 2008)

*Source*: Based on Peters (2009a).

Table 3.2 Four paradigms of the Knowledge Economy

|  | Paradigm 1 | Paradigm 2 | Paradigm 3 | Paradigm 4 |
|---|---|---|---|---|
|  | *Neoliberal Knowledge Economy* | *Network Economy* | *Creative Economy* | *Green Economy* |
| **Key actor** | Knowledge worker | Peer producer/Produser | Creative class | Green jobs |
| **Key thinker** | Machlup (1962)<br>Becker (1964)<br>Drucker (1969)<br>Bell (1973)<br>Toffler (1980)<br>Romer (1990)<br>OECD (1996) | Tapscott (1997)<br>Castells (2000)<br>Hardt & Negri (2000)<br>Benkler (2006)<br>Bruns (2008)<br>Shirky (2008)<br>Bauwens (2009) | Landry (2000)<br>Howkins (2001)<br>Robinson (2001)<br>Florida (2002a) | Daly (1996)<br>Milani (2000)<br>Jones (2008)<br>Rifkin (2011) |
| **Key themes** | Innovation, R&D, intellectual property | Peer production, mass collaboration, open source | Human ingenuity, intellectual property | Clean technologies, innovation, sustainability |
| **Key focus** | Human capital | Networked commons | Intellectual capital | Green innovation |

The purpose of this analysis is not to develop an exhaustive typology of the many paradigms of KE, but rather to consider the ways in which structural changes in advanced economies inform notions of educational reform. While each paradigm of KE represents a separate but contingent dimension of an evolving discussion on economic transformation, each paradigm also reflects unique intellectual strands in the discussion on postindustrial society. I begin with an examination of paradigm 2, the "Network Economy."

## Paradigm Two: The Network Economy

One of the more interesting features of KE theory is the debate on the "knowledge society" and the shift from mass production to knowledge-driven services. As Lyotard (1984) argues, knowledge has become the principle force of production. While knowledge may be a public good in its conceptual form, it is also now key to market economies in the form of intellectual property (IP). Notwithstanding the fact that knowledge production is poorly suited to the logic of the market, knowledge is now embedded in social and economic production by and through global information and communication technology (ICT) networks. Many scholars prefer to speak of this in terms of information capitalism (Morris-Suzuki, 1997; Castells, 2000; Hardt & Negri, 2000; Fuchs, 2005), particularly the generation, processing, and transmission of information (Castells, 2000, p. 21).

Castells (1997), for example, argues that the proper identification of an emerging global society is to be found in its networked social structure. Accordingly, the creation, distribution, and manipulation of information have converged with changes in technology, economy, and culture to produce a highly networked infrastructure. This is enacted both in terms of formal institutional organizations (including political organizations) and global and civil society more broadly. In Castells's view, the "network society" now shapes "the operation and outcomes in processes of production, experience, power, and culture," constituting the new social morphology of our time (Castells, 2000, p. 500).

Indeed, the notion of *network* has become a predominant feature of social analysis. Yochai Benkler (2006), for example, provides a strong framework for understanding changes in economic development in terms of networked production or a Network Economy (NE). Borrowing language and discourse from the open source movement (OSM), he suggests that the rise of networked environments make possible a new modality of organizing production in the form of "commons-based peer production."

In his book *The Wealth of Networks: How Social Production Transforms Markets and Freedom*, Benkler argues that peer production is an alternative to the traditional modes of organization (i.e., commercial market and bureaucratic hierarchy). Accordingly, the key to understanding networked production is that resources are held in common—that is, they are collectively shared, managed, and produced. In contrast to systems of private property, "no single person has exclusive control over the use and disposition of any particular resource in the commons" (Benkler, 2006, p. 61).

One of the central contradictions emerging with the affordances of so-called network economy/society is that it makes information easily reproducible, thus leading to a variety of freedom/control problems relating to IP. This takes the form of *copyright* for fixed creative output such as books, music, and films; *trademarks* for brand identity; *design* for product appearance; and/or *patents* for inventions. While the goal of IP protection is to incentivize creativity and invention by rewarding creative output, the rise of NE has introduced an entirely different set of values and incentives.

Where conventional notions of KE focus on the commodification of knowledge through IP regimes, advocates of NE emphasize the desirability of open source (OS) production in the context of an OSM (Leadbeater & Miller, 2004). OSM advocates argue that knowledge is a public good, linked to other commons-based resources like the natural environment. Highlighting the value of knowledge as a public good, for example, Stiglitz (1999) argues that while the logic of supply and demand suits scarce resources, knowledge lacks the materiality to be properly defined as a rival good (Romer, 1990). As a symbolic good, any number of people can construct, consume, and use knowledge without necessarily depleting its value.

According to advocates of knowledge as commons, IP is seen as preventing innovation by inhibiting the free circulation of information and ideas. The truth is that IP is a juridical concept that refers to creations of the mind for which exclusive rights are recognized.

Lessig (2004), for example, criticizes the implied analogy between physical property and IP on the grounds that while physical property may be rivalrous, intellectual works are inherently non-rivalrous (Stiglitz, 1999).

From this perspective, knowledge operates expansively to defy the normal "law" of scarcity that governs most commodity markets (Lessig, 2004). The underlying assumption here is that knowledge functions very differently from other commodities because it is neither physically manufactured, nor a rival good.

Indeed, Benkler (2006) is careful to anchor his own political arguments about NE in Kantian and Rousseauian notions of liberty in which individual autonomy is maximized through the shared ownership of resources. Indeed, Kelty (2008) describes NE as a new mode of democratization that he frames as a "recursive public." In his view, the creation and governance of knowledge and intellectual production is being revolutionized in the Age of the Internet. Kelty writes:

> A recursive public is *a public that is vitally concerned with the material and practical maintenance and modification of the technical, legal, practical, and conceptual means of its own existence as a public; it is a collective independent of other forms of constituted power and is capable of speaking to existing forms of power through the production of actually existing alternatives.* Free Software is one instance of this concept, both as it has emerged in the recent past and as it undergoes transformation and differentiation in the near future... Such publics are not inherently modifiable, but are made so—and maintained—through the practices of participants... By calling Free Software a recursive public, I am doing two things: first, I am drawing attention to the democratic and political significance of Free Software and the Internet; and second, I am suggesting that our current understanding (both academic and colloquial) of what counts as a self-governing public, or even as "the public," is radically inadequate to understanding the contemporary reorientation of knowledge and power. (pp. 3–7)

Building on this political approach, Bauwens (2009) describes NE as a new mode of peer-to-peer (P2P) production and defines P2P this way:

> I define "peer to peer" as a relational dynamic that emerges through distributed networks. Distributed networks are networks in which the structure is such that agents and nodes can take independent

action and maintain relationships "on their own," i.e. through voluntary self-aggregation and "without prior permission." It is important to look at such a network from the point of view of the human: what matters is not the purity of the structure of the distributed network," but whether or not, "in the last analysis," such self-aggregation is made possible. Self-aggregation then naturally gives rise to the emergence of peer "production"— the ability to create common value. In such a process, "peer producers" can 1) voluntary assemble capital assets, which may be material or immaterial; 2) design, through mutual adaptation, participatory governance processes ("peer governance"); and 3) simultaneously make sure that the commonly created value indeed stays "common." This is done using new forms of "common" property (i.e. neither private exclusionary nor public-collective), for which I use the term "peer property."

Bauwens develops perhaps the most comprehensive analysis of the democratic potential of NE. He concludes that NE favors networks over hierarchies, instantiating a concrete "post-Enlightenment" universalism predicated upon common projects defined in terms of (1) "open and free" availability of raw materials; (2) shared and participatory "processing"; and (3) commons-oriented output.

Accordingly, P2P processes are dynamic, but not structureless. NE structures may maintain elements of hierarchy, but their expansion is predicated upon administrative control that is "distributed" through dense clusters of linked communication. Since communication is not top-down, feedback is systemic and integrated into the protocol of the system. Whereas participants in hierarchical systems (both public and private) are organized by the "panoptism" of a political caste structure, participants within peer production systems are said to be organized by "holoptism." That is, a capacity to see the system as a whole. In principle, there is no formal filtering for participation, because "membership" is open to anyone who wishes to contribute. It is the *object of cooperation* itself that creates the temporary unity for project-based work.[1] Put differently, *equipotency* (i.e., the capacity to cooperate) is verified in the process of cooperation itself—as intelligence is not located at the center but circulates throughout the system.

The sociopolitical emphasis on equity that is often built into network models of production and consumption overlaps related principles found in political socialism and communism. The overriding idea here is that productive collaborations between knowledge workers or "cognitive labor" will make autonomy increasingly valuable to systems of production. Indeed, as Marx (1973) postulates, the evolution of technology may well undermine the capital and labor dichotomy enabling a fundamental shift in the mode of production. In Marx's view, this is an emergent function of a rising "general intellect" as a "force of production" in the reshaping of the "conditions of the process of social life" (p. 706). Building on this view, many advocates of a "socialized knowledge economy" argue that structural mutations in the growing capacities of the general intellect will eventually subsume industrial labor as the primary driver of production.

## The Rise of Open Education

While conventional systems of production depend upon closed proprietary structures, commons-based peer production utilizes open networked production to harness the creative energy of mass collaborators. Since knowledge in its immaterial or conceptual form is purely non-rivalrous, there are in fact zero marginal costs to adding more users (Stiglitz, 1999). Within the field of education, this translates as "open education" and overlaps open access (OA) science, open courseware (OCW), and open educational resources (OER).

Building on NE, the open education (OE) movement is a relatively new social phenomenon that is part of a larger trend toward openness in learning and education and is overtly linked to the affordances of digital technologies and the Internet. The term "Open Educational Resources" first came to use with the United Nations Educational, Scientific and Cultural Organisation's (UNESCO) 2002 Forum on the Impact of Open Courseware for Higher Education in Developing Countries. It was in this context that OER was first formally defined as "the open provision of educational resources, enabled by information and communication technologies, for consultation, use and adaptation by a community of users for non-commercial purposes." According to a follow-on report by the OECD (2008b), this includes

- Learning content: full courses, courseware, content modules, learning objects, collections and journals;

- Tools: software to support the development, use, reuse, and delivery of learning content, including searching and organization of content, content and learning management systems, content development tools, and online learning communities; and
- Implementation resources: IP licenses to promote open publishing of materials, design principles of best practice, and localization of content.

The concept of OE actually predates digital technologies but its significance has grown substantially with the growth of ICTs (OECD, 2007c). The OE movement itself emerges with developments in open and distance learning (ODL) in the twentieth century and is deeply tied to resource-based learning in the context of distance education.

Indeed, the connection between NE and OER is obvious. Overlapping the contemporary OS movement, OER denotes a concept that is at once legal, cultural, and economic. In fact, the OER movement has been inextricably bound to many of the same IP licensing issues confronting the OS movement from the beginning (Lessig, 2004; McMartin, 2008). This is precisely because most educational content is protected under conventional copyright. For this reason, open licensing in the form of Creative Commons has been a critical substructure to both movements. As with the OS movement, the key differentiator between OER and any other educational resource is its license. In this sense, OER is simply an educational resource that incorporates a license that facilitates reuse without first requesting permission from the copyright holder.

At the same time, the convergence between OER and Free and Open Source Software (FOSS) only occurred in the late 1990s with the expansion of an Internet-mediated culture of free sharing and peer collaboration. Hilton et al. (2010), for example, define OER in terms of the four "Rs" of openness, each R representing an increasing level of openness:

- Reuse—this is the most basic level of openness. People can use all or part of the work for their own purposes (e.g., download a copy of a song to listen to at a later time).
- Redistribute—people can share the work with others (e.g., e-mail a digital article to a colleague).

- Revise—people can modify, translate, or change the form the work takes (e.g., take a book written in English and turn it into a Spanish audio book).
- Remix—take two or more existing resources and combine them to create a new resource (e.g., take audio lectures from a course and combine them with a video from another course to create a new course).

## Paradigm Three: The Creative Economy

Beyond NE, there is another highly influential paradigm of the knowledge economy that has focused on the inordinate value of creativity and human ingenuity to social and economic growth. For the Creative Economy, competitive advantage is increasingly derived from investments in human creativity and innovation (Howkins, 2001). Tracing the contours of CE, one finds a unique discourse that both complements and undermines competing notions of KE.

In Pink's (2005) view, for example, the knowledge economy has already peaked in advanced countries and is now in fact migrating downstream to Asia and elsewhere. This is not to say that knowledge-based discovery is no longer critical to innovation but that basic logical skills are no longer sufficient to stimulate economic growth in advanced industrialized countries. This capacity (or what Pink describes as "left-brain directed" skills) are instead now present in the leading emerging economies or simply becoming embedded in ICTs.

Unlike the criticism of IP found within the NE paradigm, IP rights are viewed as foundational to CE. Where the P2P and the OS movements celebrate the commons and the widest possible latitude for shared use, CE is almost exclusively framed by the need to recoup capital investments by and through property rights. Venturelli (2005) puts it this way:

> The challenge for every nation is not how to prescribe an environment of protection for a received body of art and tradition, but how to construct one of creative explosion and innovation in all areas of the arts and sciences...Nations that fail to meet this challenge will

simply become passive consumers of ideas emanating from societies that are in fact creatively dynamic and able to commercially exploit the new creative forms. (p. 396)

For advocates of CE, copyright is the "organizing principle" and perhaps the very basis for defining postindustrial society (Towse, 2005). IP is critical to CE because it enables individual creativity to be exclusively owned and sold in the market as a key capital asset. As Howkins (2001) writes, "managing creativity involves knowing, first, when to exploit the non-rivalrous nature of ideas and, second, when to assert intellectual property rights and make one's ideas-as-products rivalrous." As he concludes: "These two decision points are the crux of the management process."

## Tracing the Creative Economy

Linking discussions on CE to broad structural mutations in the technologies underlying contemporary global capitalism, there are at least four common threads shaping the discourse on CE:

(1) the diffusion of ICTs and consequent transformations in Fordist production;
(2) the growing significance of a global market and globally fragmented production systems;
(3) the increasing importance of highly educated workers or human capital within continuous cycles of creative innovation; and
(4) the rise of alternative centers of production outside advanced industrialized countries.

Generally speaking, there are two strongly overlapping modalities for understanding what is meant by the "Creative Economy." The first modality argues that *creative industries*—and the cultural sector more broadly—represent a highly energized and growing portion of the broader economy (Hesmondhalgh, 2002; Hartley, 2005). The second modality argues that creativity is as an *axial principle* underlying postindustrial shifts linked to globalization (Florida, 2002a).

Looking at both modalities in detail, we see significant differences of scale.

## Creative Industries

The first modality of CE is linked to discussions on "creative industries" and includes industries overlapping publishing, music, visual/performing arts, film, media, architecture, advertising, and design. Since the 1990s, policymakers and intergovernmental organizations such as UNESCO have developed fairly elaborate definitions of creative industries in the context of broader national innovation strategy. Indeed, the evolution of the terms "cultural industries" and "creative industries" has been traced fairly extensively (Cunningham, 2001; Hesmondhalgh, 2002; Hesmondhalgh & Pratt, 2005) and is underpinned by a diversity of policy initiatives. In fact, the idea of creative industries has existed for some time, beginning with Adorno and Horkheimer's (1944/1977) early neo-Marxist critiques of mass media and the "culture industry" and evolving through a complex, though highly contested discourse on the nature and function of art and culture in the global economy.[2]

Cunningham (2001) distinguishes between the culture industries and creative industries this way: where the "classic" cultural industries are a product of the technological advances of the early twentieth century, the creative industries arise from the technological change of the late twentieth and early twenty-first centuries. In this new revised view, culture is abandoned as elitist and exclusive, while "creativity" is embraced as democratic and inclusive (Galloway & Dunlop, 2007, p. 19). Much of this thinking builds on a rejection of class-based distinctions between the cultural industries–produced for commercial entertainment (film, publishing, and music), and the subsidized "arts" (visual and performing arts, museums, and galleries) (Horkheimer & Adorno, 2002).

Interestingly, while developed economies produce and consume the lion's share of the global market in creative products and services, many developing countries, particularly countries in Asia, are beginning to see growing returns. One striking example of this emerging pattern is the increasing dominance of Asia in the area of technology-related creative goods, such as computers, cameras, televisions, and audiovisual equipment. From 1996 to 2005, exports in these key industries grew from $51 billion to $274 billion (UNCTAD, 2008, p. 6). Not surprisingly, China has (since 2005) become the world's leading producer and exporter of value-added creative products.

What is interesting is that creative industries today are estimated to be growing globally at an average rate of 8.7 percent per year (UNCTAD, 2008, p. 24). US creative industries (defined in terms of arts, media, and design), for example, are estimated to make up 8 percent of the national GDP, outstripping auto production, aircraft production, agriculture, electronics, and computer technologies (Siwek, 2002). In fact, the annual growth rate of creative industries in OECD countries during the 1990s was twice that of the service industries overall and four times that of manufacturing overall (Howkins, 2001, p. xvi). Indeed, world exports of visual arts more than doubled from $10.3 billion in 1996 to $22.1 billion in 2005. Between 2000 and 2005, world trade in creative goods and services reached $424.4 billion in 2005, or 3.4 percent of the total world trade.

> World exports of creative products were valued at $424.4 billion in 2005 as compared to $227.5 billion in 1996, according to preliminary UNCTAD figures. Creative services in particular enjoyed rapid export growth—8.8. per cent annually between 1996 and 2005. This positive trend occurred in all regions and groups of countries and is expected to continue into the next decade, assuming that the global demand for creative goods and services continues to rise. (UNCTAD, 2008, p. iv)

The major challenge for understanding CE in terms of creative industries, however, lies in defining the depth and scope of those industries. The truth is that creative industries employ a relatively small percentage of the workforce. In the United States, for example, creative industries account for less than 10 percent of total employment. Indeed, "if we interpret the cultural economy as a sector (including, e.g., Hollywood, television, the arts, design, fashion) it is vibrant and significant, but not nearly significant enough in job creation to make up for the millions of jobs lost in manufacturing and through outsourcing" (Nederveen Pieterse, 2010, p. 413).

## Creativity as Axial Principle

The second modality for understanding CE is much broader and more diffuse. It views creativity as vital to the economy in general and fundamental to an innovation-driven global economy in particular. Following this line of reasoning, Howkins (2001) and Florida (2002a) make creativity the axial principle of a postindustrial society. Underlying this version of CE is an argument that creativity is now the key driver of global innovation (Christensen, 1997). Creativity is not in itself an economic activity however, but only becomes an economic activity "when it produces an idea with economic implications or a tradable product" (Howkins, 2001, p. x). Florida (2002a), in particular, makes the argument that a new creative class made up of intellectuals, artists, and designers is an ascendant force in reshaping advanced capitalist economies. Building out from a "creative class" of scientists, engineers, architects, designers, musicians, artists, educators, and entertainers, CE is understood to constitute 30 percent of the US workforce (with a "supercreative" core representing only 12% and a larger contingent of creative professionals in business, finance, health, law, accounting, and related professions representing 18%). Florida elaborates,

> In 1900, creative workers made up only about 10 percent of the U.S. workforce. By 1980, that figure had risen to nearly 20 percent. Today, almost 40 million workers—some 30 percent of the workforce—are employed in the creative sector.... When we divide the economy into three sectors—the creative, manufacturing and service sectors—and add up all the wages and salaries paid, the creative sector accounts for nearly half of all wage and salary income in the United States. That's nearly $2 trillion, almost as much as manufacturing and services combined. (Florida, 2007, pp. 29–30)

Much of this discussion elides with a multifaceted discourse on urbanization and the rise of a global urban elite. In contrast to Friedman's (2005) notion of a "flat world," for example, Florida (2007: xviii) argues that wealth and power is becoming increasingly concentrated within the world's richest cities (Sassen, 1991). This is not a minor point. Indeed, while the share of the world's population living in urban areas was just 3 percent in 1800, and 30 percent in 1950, it is 50 percent today and as high as 75 percent in advanced capitalist countries. In fact, the world's 40 largest mega-regions are now home to some 18 percent of the world's population and produce two-thirds of global economic output (including nearly nine in ten new patented innovations).

As Florida concludes, while flat world theories of globalization accurately register the rising influence of emerging economies like India and China, they overlook the growing divide between the super-educated and the vast majority who lack access to education. In truth, it is not that the world has become "flatter" but the world's economic peaks have become slightly more dispersed.

Indeed, for Florida, it is the world's global cities that anchor CE and enable the financial and commercial power of the creative class. Housed within the world's global cities, the rising creative class operate at the peak of social and economic power. Accordingly, economic peaks like New York, Paris, London, and Tokyo form the major control nodes of the global economy (Porter, 1990; Sassen, 1991).

Alongside other discourses on postindustrial society advocates of CE argue that capitalist economies are entering into a new world, a world in which the major raw materials are no longer coal and steel produced by machines, but creativity and innovation produced by the human imagination. In this way, CE is framed as both an empirical study of current changes within capitalist economy and a policy forecast of increasing changes to come. Accordingly, a country's cultural capacity for openness or tolerance is seen as critical to future prosperity (Florida, 2002a). Tolerance for diversity and "low barriers to entry" attract and absorb skilled talent while supporting the rich environments that stoke creative innovation. Much of this thinking builds on the work of Jane Jacobs (1961, 1969). Drawing a correlation between diversity and innovation, for example, Jacobs emphasized the role of cities and regions as platforms for the assimilation and diffusion of knowledge (Sassen, 1991). Indeed, building on Jacobs's work, Lucas (1998) highlights the clustering effect of human capital, focusing on the capacity of cities to localize and reduce the cost of knowledge transfer to enable ideas and new knowledge to arise and circulate more efficiently. As the scale and diversity of cities increase, so do the number of connections generating new ideas and innovation.

If Florida and other advocates of CE are right, then creativity is now fundamental to wealth and prosperity and cultural innovation is critical to its flourishing. Yet it is precisely creativity that is least valued by contemporary educational institutions.

The truth is that the vast majority of educational organizations today deliberately submerge creativity beneath layers of command-and-control. While it was once true that school systems effectively distributed the necessary skills for an age of industry (numeracy, literacy, symbol manipulation), it is equally true that these same institutions are not equipped to support the skills and capacities for an age of creative innovation.

## Paradigm Four: The Green Economy

The fourth paradigm of the knowledge economy that I examine is the Green Economy (GE). Building on concern about climate change and the impact of carbon dioxide emissions, GE is both an economic discourse and a political discourse emphasizing the need for closed loop economic policies. While the concept of GE is largely associated with minimal or no waste production of goods and services, the definition of GE remains in flux. According to the UN, GE "seeks, in principle, to unite under a single banner the entire suite of economic policies and modes of economic analyses of relevance to sustainable development" (UN DESA, 2010, p. 15). This includes advances in technological innovation, renewable energy generation (wind, solar, geothermal, and biomass) and energy conservation. In theory, GE translates as improved human well-being and social equity, while at the same time significantly reducing environmental risks and ecological scarcities (UNEP, 2014).

Linked to the elimination of fossil fuels and a long-term transformation of highly polluting industrial industries to low-carbon, low-waste industries, GE is viewed by many as an oxymoron (Lander, 2011; Brand, 2012). This is because the massive resource-driven exploitation inherent to capitalist production contradicts the basic principles of ecological sustainability (Daly and Farley, 2010). Indeed, McMurtry (1999) describes the current phase of global economic development as the "cancer phase" of capitalism. In his view, the globalization of laissez-faire capitalism is not merely analogous to cancer but is in fact a real and growing disease that threatens the capacity of the planet's social and cellular immune systems.

## The Green Economy and Public Policy

For advocates of green policy, reducing global warming and enhancing resource management are critical to developing GE. In their view, the evidence from climate science points to the need for a large-scale and coordinated response to climate change, including broad portfolios of active technologies and regulatory policies. In United States, for example, the rising call for green innovation has stimulated interest in the potential of rejuvenating the economy through "green jobs." The International Labour Organization (ILO) defines green jobs as those that improve energy and raw materials efficiency, limit greenhouse gas emissions, minimize waste and pollution, protect and restore ecosystems, and support adaptation to the effects of climate change (ILO, 2009). Van Jones (2008), for example, has proposed a *Green New Deal* in the United States that seeks to transform the country's economy around low- and medium-skill "green collar" jobs. At the enterprise level, this would likely include green buildings or clean transportation, the reduction of resource consumption, or improvement in recycling systems.

Most theorists point to the need for developing an electricity-driven smart grid as the backbone for GE. This is because the challenge underlying any strategy for renewable energy generation directly overlaps the need for enhancing energy storage and transmission. Changes to the US electricity grid, for example, would mean introducing next generation digital technologies in the development of a national smart grid.

This also includes structural changes in electricity management that could directly reshape the relationship between suppliers (utilities) and customers. A two-way power flow from distributed renewables like solar and wind, for example, would mean that consumers could sell excess electricity back to the grid. Using smart grids, US energy production could become augmented by clusters of locally distributed energy resources (DER). While DER systems are small-scale power-generation technologies (typically in the range of 3–10,000 kW), they could be combined to form dense clusters of networked energy. Since most forms of renewables (ocean tide, wind, solar) are inherently variable or intermittent, smart grids offer the capacity to balance sudden drops in electrical generation by adjusting storage and consumption.

In fact, the rush of stimulus spending during the 2008 economic crisis included significant investments in GE. The administration's stimulus bill dedicated $71 billion to clean energy funding, with an additional $20 billion for loan guarantees and tax incentives to support clean energy projects. This included a proposed investment in high-capacity transmission that spans the country, linking local electric utilities and distantly located bulk power generation to a Unified National Smart Grid. Using advanced, high-voltage lines, the US Unified Smart Grid has been envisioned as efficiently moving electricity across vast geographic distances with minimal losses.

At the same time, green energy pilot projects in the United States remain disconnected and isolated. Rifkin (2011: 34), for example, is particularly critical of President Obama's green policies, which he argues lack a vision for a networked energy era. Rather than taking advantage of distributed infrastructure, the philosophy shaping US green policies remains fixed to centralized energy transmission. More than a collection of point-to-point interconnections between regional systems, the Unified National Smart Grid is necessarily a multidirectional electrical transmission platform, enabling access points to function as virtual power generators or grid energy storage facilities. Deploying a unified energy network on a national scale could mean that consumers also become producers, collaborating over an open energy grid (Von Hippel, 2005; Bauwens, 2009). Taken as a whole, this means the addition of new layers of advanced technology onto the US smart grid, bridging adjacent markets in architectural design, smart home appliances, wireless networks, auto production, and traditional utilities.

## Infrastructure for the Green Economy

In his recent book, *The Third Industrial Revolution* (2011), Rifkin argues that the promise of GE represents the rise of a new kind of development rooted in an "energy internet" or *intergrid* that he believes is emerging as a mega-platform for a post-carbon civilization. Where the twentieth century was powered by oil, and the nineteenth century powered by coal and steam, Rifkin argues that the twenty-first century will be powered by distributed renewables such as solar, wind, hydro, geothermal heat, biomass, and ocean tide. The key to GE, he believes, is leveraging the affordances of ICTs as an infrastructure for networked consumption and production.

As he explains, smart grids will eventually enable green energy to replace a centralized carbon-based energy industry, allowing prosumers to generate their own power. This is linked to the convergence of the Internet with an embryonic Energy Internet and a Logistics Internet or Internet of Things (IoT). Much as the steam-powered printing press enabled the necessary communication infrastructure for managing the First Industrial Revolution, and the telephone enabled the massive centralization and communication infrastructure for the Second Industrial Revolution, so the Internet is understood as the necessary network infrastructure for managing and coordinating the Third Industrial Revolution. As Rifkin explains, the "telephone, radio and television were centralized forms of communications designed to manage and market an economy organized around centralized fossil fuel energies and the myriad business practices that flowed from that energy regime" (p. 20). By contrast, the "new, second-generation electricity communication... is distributed in nature and ideally suited to manage distributed forms of energy" (pp. 20–21). He elaborates:

> In the 1990s and the first decade of the twenty-first century, the Information and Communication Technology (ICT) revolution was grafted onto the older, centralized Second Industrial Revolution. It was, from the start, an unnatural fit. While ICT enhanced productivity, streamlined practices and created some new business opportunities and jobs—which probably extended the useful life of an aging industrial model—it could never achieve its full distributed communications potential because of the inherent constraints that come with being attached to a centralized energy regime and commercial infrastructure. (p. 20)

Building on the P2P architecture of the Network Economy, Rifkin describes the coming GE as essentially a democratic energy commons that is largely free to produce and consume. Supported by five major institutional pillars, he argues that the collaborative logic of this green energy regime has begun entirely reshaping the command-and-control superstructure of industrial society. Accordingly, the pillars of GE include:

1. *A shift to renewable energy*—including solar, wind, hydro, geothermal, ocean waves, and biomass.
2. *The design of buildings as power plants*—the design and construction of buildings as independent power generators or "power plants" from the sun, wind, and waste to provide for their own power needs as well as surplus energy that can be shared.
3. *Deploying hydrogen and other storage technologies in every building and throughout the infrastructure to store intermittent energies*—the use of hydrogen as a universal medium that "stores" all forms of renewable energy to assure that a stable and reliable supply is available for power generation and transmission.
4. *Using Internet technology to transform the power grid of every continent into an energy-sharing intergrid like the Internet*—the development of a "smart grid" or "intergrid" as a mega-platform, enabling businesses and homeowners to produce their own energy and share surplus power (much as information is produced and shared other across the Internet).
5. *Transitioning the transport fleet to electric, plug-in, and fuel cell vehicles that can buy and sell electricity on a smart continental interactive power grid.* In support of these five pillars, Rifkin points to the need for government leadership in the area of green policies to provide the basic resources (capital, tax incentives, etc.) and ideological support to advance and coordinate industries across a wide range of sectors. Joining a wide swath of industries that include clean technologies, green design and construction, telecommunication, fuel cell and plug-in transport, nanotechnology, and supply chain logistics, is the growing potential of advancing technologies.

## Smart Cities

Underlying discussions on technological innovation for GE is the application of "smart technologies" to a range of ICT-driven services supporting "smart cities". As a recent OECD (2013b) report explains, smart technologies refer to applications or services that are "able to learn from previous situations and to communicate the results of these situations to other devices and users" (p. 4). Commonly portrayed as the next stage in Internet technologies, smart technologies include:

1. Machine-to-Machine (M2M) communication across mobile devices.
2. Large-scale data processing via "Cloud Computing" to process and display data.
3. Data analytics or "Big Data" to correlate and interpret data.

Building on layers of fixed Internet protocol networks, "always on" broadband networks, and, more recently, wireless satellite and mobile networks, smart cities increasingly leverage massive amounts of data generated by billions of Internet and mobiles devices and services around the world. The key feature of smart cities is the capacity to respond to feedback generated through data in order to change the action or behavior of a system or subsystem. Accordingly, smart cities are emergent wholes made up of interdependent subsystems of networked resources that together afford scaled "intelligence":

> Systems can be scaled up, from individual units that are smart, to combinations of devices that make a larger whole smart. A smart household might combine a smart energy metre, smart lighting, smart thermostats, alarm system with applications on mobile phones, interaction with televisions and so forth. A smart energy grid can consist of smart energy metres in people's homes, smart loading stations for electric cars, smart distribution networks and many others. Smart transport needs smart automobiles, smart delivery vehicles and logistical systems, smart public transport and smart roads working together. The better interconnected these independent units and separate systems are, the "smarter" the larger set could be considered. (OECD, 2013b, p. 9)

Taken as a whole, the growing potential of smart technologies to reshape urban development are significant. Estimates are that there will be between 20 and 50 billion devices connected to the Internet between 2020 and 2030 as Moore's law continues to drive resource costs down and capabilities up (OECD, 2013b, p. 10). Much of this technological infrastructure will be embedded within information systems that enable the transmission, storage, and processing, of Big Data.

With urban investment forecast to grow in excess of $40 trillion dollars over the next 25 years, smart cities may well represent the first new industry of the twenty-first century (Townsend, 2014). In fact, new opportunities for skilled and semiskilled labor should be more common as digital technologies begin to reshape urban development. While labor opportunities are expanding fastest in emerging economies—especially the BRIC countries—new investments in smart cities are increasingly impacting urbanization across advanced economies as well. In the United States, this amounts to $2 trillion in spending and investment (Townsend, 2014, p. 30).

For many theorists on GE, smart cities are critical to policy and planning for slowing and even reversing climate change. Cities constitute only 2 percent of the earth's surface, however, they generate a staggering 70 percent of greenhouse-gas emissions. Considering the growing importance of cities to human development, this is not a minor concern. With over half of the world's population now living in cities and forecasts of 70 percent of the world's population moving to cities by 2050, smart cities may well be pivotal to the future of postindustrial societies.

Indeed, the growing discussion on smart cities in relation to human capital is particularly important to rethinking social policy. Beyond technology (2008), Hollands argues for a vision of smart cities that bridges the discourse on creativity and human development. As he suggests, the key to truly smart cities is the capacity of ICT networks to support social capital and sociocultural development. The real basis for smart cities, in other words, begins with people. As Campbell (2012, p. 9) observes,

> it is not surprising that cities should be entering a global hunt for knowledge. It can be (and has been) argued that very *raison d'etre* of cities is that they facilitate exchange of all kinds. More to the point, in a globalized economy where knowledge plays an increasing role, cities are the crucibles where linkages are made. In turn, linkages are the channels of learning, and learning is a key not only to good practice, but also to creating wealth and reducing poverty among the poorest.

## Beyond Quantitative Growth

Interestingly, Milani (2000) suggests that GE represents the emergence of a kind of post-capitalist society based around principles of design, regeneration, and sustainability. Drawing a distinction between the current economic focus on capitalist-driven quantitative growth and a long-term shift toward dematerialization he describes GE in terms of an economic focus on qualitative development (Daly and Farley, 2010). As he explains, the substitution of human intelligence for materials, energy, and cognitive labor is part of a "dematerialization" of production and a shift toward an economics of human potential (p. 72). Put differently, this shift toward "people production" is part and parcel of the decline of industrial civilization and the waning of neoliberalism.

Much as Bauwens (2009), Milani links the affordances of network technologies to a new era of democratization and stochastic systems that he argues depend on self-organization and coordination from below. Milani explains it this way:

> The organic character of postindustrial organization suggests a trend towards growing democracy. It implies that political consciousness and control must be more integrated into everyday work life... These trends are enhanced by the impact of electronic communications technology, which makes possible the coordination of widely decentralized units. Authentic postindustrialism therefore facilitates direct democracy... Network organization allows the creation of "communities of communities." The extension of our minds and nervous systems through new communications technologies—which today is most often used to reinforce centralized control—is actually more appropriately used to empower communities and regions, allowing them to be integrated with nature's bioregions. (pp. 73–74)

Criticizing arguments that fetishize "information" as a new mode of economic development (Castells, 2000), he argues that information technology should play a subordinate role in the development of a qualitative economy that is largely focused on human social development (p. 154).

Indeed, most advocates of GE build on a critique of neoliberalism, and argue for the need to transform economic development around education, community development, and environmental stewardship. Perhaps, most importantly, they point to the need for linking creativity and cultural production (CE) to green innovation. In contrast to the mechanical systems of a "paleotechnic era" (Lyle, 1994), for example, Milani argues that an evolving economy and society is beginning to mirror the complex systems found in nature. In his view, this new era involves both designing new sociotechnical systems based on natural systems (biomimicry), and provisioning long-term investments in human ingenuity and technological innovation. "Complex systems," Milani writes, whether "production systems or whole economies, literally must be allowed to evolve, like ecosystems" (p. 73). Indeed, underlying the vision of GE is the ideal of a reconstituted society that mirrors the ecological complexity found in nature.

## Conclusion

Notwithstanding the various features that distinguish the paradigms of KE, it would not be an oversimplification to point out that all four paradigms pay close attention to the issue of human capital. For both KE and GE, human capital elides with STEM skills and represents a kind of measure of labor quality. For CE, human capital is more properly associated with creativity and ideas, and linked to a growing discussion on entrepreneurship and IP. For NE, human capital is viewed with suspicion and elides with notions of social practice and social capital in the context of peer production. While conventional measures of human capital are largely based on educational attainment (i.e., the share of a population with postsecondary education), knowledge and learning in the context of networks are tightly embedded in communities-of-practice. This kind of distinction is particularly significant, for example, to theories on educational evaluation and assessment.

While there are substantial differences between the Neoliberal Knowledge Economy, the Network Economy, the Creative Economy, and the Green Economy, there are many corresponding features as well. Overlapping all four paradigms, for example, is a rich discussion on innovation as a foundation to socioeconomic transformation.

Indeed, what most closely ties all four paradigms together is a shared social imaginary that forecasts the future. Though differing in emphasis, each of these paradigms reflects an eschatological approach to history that aims at prefiguring the future evolution of human society (Barbrook, 2006).

Taken as a whole, all four paradigms share intellectual roots in a historical metanarrative that links forecasts on social development to a leading vanguard or "remnant" (Barbrook, 2006). Oscillating between a "new ruling class" and a "new working class" is a common vision of coming economic salvation. Building on rhetoric of future utopia, all four paradigms are sustained by soteriological narratives of elite formation. This same rhetoric underlies other related theories on elite formation such as Adam Smith's "Philosophers of Industry" (1776), Karl Marx's "Proletariat" (1848), Max Weber's "Bureaucrats" (1922/1978), Frederick Taylor's "Scientific Managers" (1911/1967), Joseph Schumpeter's "Entrepreneurs" (1942/1976), Peter Drucker's "Knowledge Workers" (1969), Daniel Bell's "Knowledge Class" (1973), Alvin Toffler's "Prosumers" (1980), Jean-Francois Lyotard's "Postmodernists" (1984), and more recently Richard Florida's (2002) "Creative Class."

Beyond their similarities, there are particular features and characteristics that divide these paradigms as well. On close inspection, we see that each paradigm emphasizes a unique element of KE. For example, each paradigm differs on its assumptions about innovation, about the logics of production and consumption, and about the political economy of labor. In fact, what is perhaps most problematic about these varied discourses on KE is the lack of a substantial political critique. From the standpoint of critical theory, for example, only NE offers a detailed analysis of social exploitation within capitalist economy. Indeed, while it may be true that a rising creative minority can make its living as the vanguard of a social and technological revolution, the truth is that this is largely the result of services afforded by the mundane labor of subordinate social classes (Barbrook, 2006). In the next chapter I examine public documents produced by the Obama administration with the purpose of further unpacking assumptions about KE that now inform US educational policy.

# Chapter 4

# Education Policy and the Obama Administration

In the previous chapters I examined the economic underpinnings of US education policy. Against a historic background of neoliberal social policies, I have argued that recent debates about US education are framed by economic theories focused on the pursuit of human capital formation across a changing economic landscape. In the chapter that follows, I examine public documents introduced by the Obama administration and offer a critical analysis of these documents. These documents include:

(1) *A Strategy for American Innovation: Securing Our Economic Growth and Prosperity*, National Economic Council, Council of Economic Advisers, and Office of Science and Technology Policy, 2011
(2) *A Blueprint for Reform: The Reauthorization of the Elementary and Secondary Education Act*, US Department of Education, 2010a
(3) *Transforming American Education: Learning Powered by Technology, National Education Technology Plan*, US Department of Education, 2010c

Notwithstanding the fact that the State is responsible for designing and steering national policies, the State is itself buttressed by policy discourses that circulate through a global network of institutions and agencies (Rizvi and Lingard, 2010). Discourses that frame education policy today are no longer fused to the state, but "emanate from international and supranational organizations such as the Organization for Economic Cooperation and Development (OECD), the World Bank and the European Union (EU)" (Rizvi and Lingard, 2010, p. 14). These organizations now play a substantial role in affecting the broader discourse shaping the goals and purposes of national education systems. Consequently, public policy is now interwoven with a broad range of international policymaking networks that are multilayered (Slaughter, 2004) and informed by socioeconomic changes across local, national, and global sites.

Throughout this book, I make the argument that unpacking US education policy requires a careful appreciation of the history of NIS strategy and the pervasive influence of economic theory in guiding educational reform. Over the past century US innovation strategy has explicitly used macroeconomic theory to justify investments in education (Mazzucato, 2011). More recently, economic policies building on endogenous growth theory have focused NIS strategy on the need for competitive human capital. What is clear from these documents is that rising demand for skilled labor is not simply rooted in a temporary economic downturn, but in a permanent sea change in the structure of the global economy.

Indeed, the downward pressure resulting from expanding global competition has provoked educational reform measures that are obsessively focused on improving the quality of the US labor force. Even a cursory analysis of contemporary US education policy reveals a deep concern with transforming education in the face of daunting challenges linked to globalization. Much as previous administrations, the Obama administration has aimed at raising the quality of public education through federal reforms in order to boost economic performance. This federalization of US education has also included new accountability systems linking teacher evaluation and remuneration to standardized testing.

Response to these reforms among educationalists has largely been negative. Ambitious attempts to transform public education through the expansion of charter schools, for example, has been met with accusations of classism. Scholars point out that many of the reforms introduced by the Obama administration fail to address the root causes of social inequality (National Center for Education Statistics, 2011). In the view of critical scholars, education systems today remain mired in the reproduction of class structure (Freire, 1970; Bowles and Gintis, 1976; Bourdieu, 1998; Apple, 2006; McLaren, 2007). Indeed, the strongest criticism of President Obama's educational policies is that they are driven by political ideologies geared to serving the interests of a "transnational capitalist class" (Sklair, 2001).

## A Strategy for American Innovation: Securing Our Economic Growth and Prosperity

Building on NIS theory, *A Strategy for American Innovation* (Whitehouse, 2011) represents the Obama administration's proposal for advancing US economic policy. Composed by the National Economic Council, the Council of Economic Advisers, and the Office of Science and Technology Policy, *A Strategy for American Innovation* (SAI) emphasizes the role of government in steering the US innovation system:

> By championing policies that facilitate marketplace innovation, the federal government will continue to be an essential partner in the U.S. national innovation system. To that end, the Obama administration will take appropriate public action by supporting an environment in which innovation is rewarded and best practices are diffused, investing in a technically capable workforce, supporting basic scientific discoveries, and promoting the development of the technology platforms from which future innovations will spring. Government direction can never be a substitute for the free market conditions that propel American innovation. But government must act to support those conditions and ensure that innovation, the engine of our prosperity, drives America further and faster towards higher quality jobs, healthier and longer lives, new opportunities and new industries, and the ever-expanding technological frontier. (p. 13)

Focusing less on individual technologies and more on the wider processes of innovation, NIS policy under President Obama is grounded in a working assumption that public investment in innovation is critical to catalyzing the US economy. SAI summarizes its argument for public investment this way:

> In areas of well-defined national importance, public investments can help catalyze advances, leveraging key breakthroughs and U.S. leadership. The 21st century brings several critical areas—including energy, bio- and nanotechnology, space capabilities, health care, and education—where the demand for breakthroughs is clear. The Administration's Strategy for American Innovation will harness public mechanisms to help meet our common goals, sparking commercial innovations and American ingenuity as we seek to meet the grand challenges of the next century and add impressive new chapters to the history of American progress. (p. 25)

Positioning the role of government in the US economy as an "innovation facilitator," SAI makes the case for neo-Keynesian policy reforms beginning with wide-ranging investments in the "building blocks" of innovation. SAI defines innovation as "the process by which individuals and organizations generate new ideas and put them into practice" (p. 7). Accordingly, innovation strategy proceeds in developmental stages:

> First, we must create an educational system that is internationally competitive and innovative in preparing our workforce for our increasingly knowledge-intensive economy. Next, we must invest in scientific research to restore America's leadership in creating the scientific and technological breakthroughs that underpin private sector innovations. Finally, we must invest in a first-class infrastructure that moves people and ideas at 21st century speeds. These are the building blocks of an innovation strategy that will lead America to a more prosperous future. (p. 15)

US Innovation strategy is conceptualized as a pyramid of embedded layers supporting rising innovation, economic investment, and growth (figure 4.1). These layers include:

1. Investments in the "building blocks of innovation" (education, R&D, and infrastructure).

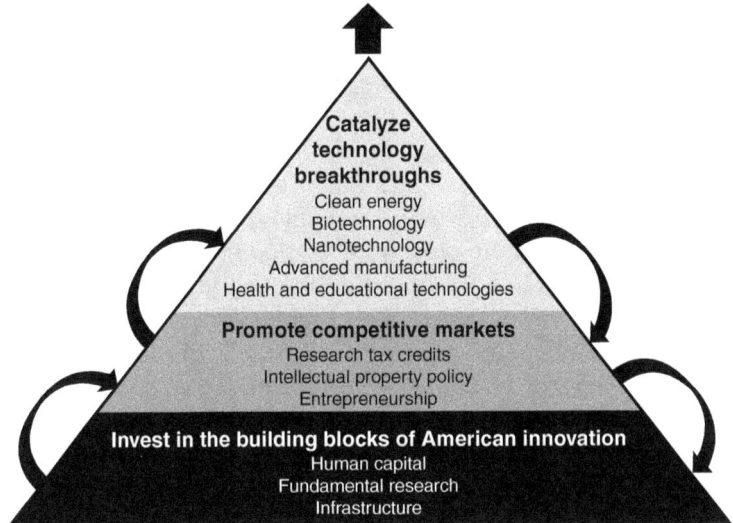

**Figure 4.1** US innovation strategy.
*Source*: Adapted from Whitehouse (2011).

2. Promotion of competitive markets through entrepreneurship, export promotion, and regional cluster strategies.
3. Catalyzation of technology breakthroughs in clean energy, health care technologies, education technology, and advanced manufacturing.

Investments in Innovation

The foundation layer of SAI includes basic investments that seed follow-on development. These investments include:

1. Reform of K-12 education and workforce training (with a special emphasis on STEM fields).
2. Increased funding for basic scientific research.
3. Increased physical infrastructure investments (including proposals for high-speed rail and a National Infrastructure Bank).

4. Increased "virtual" infrastructure investments (including the Internet, a new smart grid, expanded wireless spectrum, and cyberspace security).

Taken together, these investments form the foundations of several government-led initiatives, including: (i) expanded commercial spectrum in support of wireless technology; (ii) patent reform to modernize and speed up the administration of patent applications; (iii) improvements in K-12 education through research institutions (ARPA-ED), competitive funding, public-private partnerships, and an increased number of STEM teachers; (iv) funding for clean energy research (ARPA-E), higher energy standards, and the renewal of clean energy tax credits; (v) support for early-stage entrepreneurship via new funding systems (Startup America) and improvements in the regulatory environment.

## Market Promotion

The second layer of the Obama administration's NIS pyramid is a focus on market promotion to support innovation through government oversight. Markets are seen as platforms through which innovations can diffuse globally and scale across industries. Market promotion policies include:

1. Research and Experimentation Tax Credits to accelerate innovation ($100 billion over 10 years).
2. Various initiatives to ease entrepreneurship (patent reform, Startup America, the Affordable Care Act).
3. Bridging new and established entrepreneurs through "innovation hubs."
4. Improving regulation and market access both domestically and globally via advocacy and policy.

## Catalyze Breakthroughs for National Priorities

At the peak of the NIS policy pyramid is public investment in R&D. Government is seen as a major driver of new experimental technologies coordinating public-private partnership (green technology, health care technology, educational technology, biotechnology, and nanotechnology). This includes:

1. New clean energy standards and investments in clean energy research.
2. Research institutions in biotechnology, nanotechnology, and advanced manufacturing.
3. Next-generation applications for space (communication, navigation, commerce, and security).
4. Health care technologies (health IT, data) to improve quality care.
5. Next-generation educational technologies to personalize learning and advance lifelong learning and training.

Emphasizing State entrepreneurship (Mazzucato, 2011), SAI argues that the "true choice in innovation policy" is not between government management or no government management (i.e. neoliberalism), but rather the "right role for government" (p. 10). However, even as SAI makes an overt argument for shaping US public policy around a pronounced NIS framework, it remains inwardly focused on domestic concerns. (National Intelligence Council, 2012). As Bauer (2012) observes, this approach may prove counterproductive in a global knowledge economy.

## SAI and Education Policy

SAI does a laudable job of conveying the challenges posed by KE, especially the need for creative problem-solving skills (table 4.1). While only a small percentage of students needed advanced skills in the industrial era, today a capacity to apply knowledge to solve problems is seen as a basic perquisite to accessing a global labor market (Dede, 2013). More than "skills" per se, there is an increasing need for students to experiment with applying knowledge in the practice of creative and entrepreneurial problem-solving (Zhao, 2012b). In fact, SAI underscores this point arguing that the historic strength

**Table 4.1**  Strategy for American innovation

---

- Improve America's science, technology, engineering, and math (STEM) education, including preparation of an additional 100 thousand STEM teachers (by the end of the decade) through public-private partnerships and organizations like Educate to Innovate and Change the Equation
- Reform elementary and secondary education by steering state and local K-12 educational reform through the use of competitive grants (Race to the Top) and federal educational policy reform (Blueprint for Reform)
- Restore America to first in the world in college attainment through expansion of the Pell Grant program ($40 billion), the Health Care and Education Reconciliation Act (making all federal loans available directly to students rather than third-party administrators), the American Opportunity Tax Credit (worth $10,000 for four years of college), the Trade Adjustment Act (investing in community colleges), and the Task Force on Skills for America's Future (bridging businesses and educational institutions)
- Create a first-class system of early education by investing in early childhood development, reforming Head Start programs through competitive funding (the Early Learning Challenge Fund) through common standards and quality improvement

---

*Source*: Based on Whitehouse (2011).

of the US economy has been its explicit focus on entrepreneurship. Despite this recognition, however, the principle of entrepreneurship itself is not reflected in the substance of educational reforms. The notion that the US education system may need to reconsider the factory transmission model itself, for example, is entirely absent.

## Education Reform in Context

Building on NIS strategy, there are specific reasons that US education policy is now directly tied to concerns around economic planning. Notwithstanding the considerable political and economic power of the United States, its relative position in the world has been declining for some time. Alongside a chronic dependence on low interest rates, and a belief that monetary policy can regulate the economy, GDP growth is now driven by consumption and government deficit (Marber, 2014).

Deterioration in US economic power has been most apparent in the trade data. Weak manufacturing (deindustrialization) has led to a massive trade deficit, import dependence, and a protracted trade and current account deficit (Nederveen Pieterse, 2012). US share of world merchandise exports has fallen from 17 percent in 1963 to less than 9 percent today, even as US share of imports has expanded from less than 9 percent to 13 percent (Mandel, 2012). Even as the United States remains the largest economy in the world, it has also become the largest debtor nation. Highly dependent on other countries—especially China—to consume its treasury bonds, US reliance on foreign capital has lead to a succession of economic bubbles, including the dotcom bubble, the low interest bubble, the real estate bubble, and, mostly recently, the subprime mortgage crisis.

Indeed, educational reform is a very small part of a very large problem. Consider, for example, the scale of challenges confronting the Obama administration upon entering office. Responding to the highest unemployment rate in 30 years, two very expensive and unpopular wars in the Middle East, and the failure and/or collapse of some of the largest financial institutions in the world (Bear Sterns, Lehman Brothers, and AIG), the first term of the Obama administration was largely subsumed with stabilization policy. In response to the devastating damage of the Great Recession, the Obama administration introduced five pillars for stabilizing the US economy: (1) greater regulation of Wall Street and the disproportionate influence of finance capitalism; (2) investments in education in order to prepare students for the twenty-first century; (3) promotion and investment in clean energy technologies (and a corresponding reduction in Middle Eastern oil); (4) reform of the health care system; (5) a reduction in the national deficit in the development of a sustainable US economy.

Building on top of the Bush administration's $700 billion banking bailout known as the Troubled Asset Relief Program (TARP), President Obama introduced an additional $787 billion fiscal stimulus package in the form of the American Recovery and Reinvestment Act (ARRA)[1]. Aimed at rescuing the United States from a deepening global recession, and combined with an assortment of tax cuts, ARRA provided funding for a wide array of spending initiatives intended to stimulate the US economy. Distributed over several years, ARRA included increased federal spending[2] for health care, infrastructure, and education (table 4.2), as well as highly articulated reforms to social policy. Of the $787 billion in stimulus, close to $100 billion was designated for aid to public education (P-16), including $48.6 billion in a state fiscal stabilization fund, $39.75 billion available to local districts and higher education institutions, and $8.8 billion for facilities' modernization and repair (table 4.3).

**Table 4.2** Actual ARRA spending during the period 2009–2011 (in billions)

| Department/Agency | Estimated 2009–2011 | Actual 2009–2011 | Difference Actual minus Estimate |
|---|---|---|---|
| Agriculture | 20.0 | 31.3 | +11.3 |
| Commerce | 4.5 | 3.3 | −1.2 |
| Defense–Military Programs | 6.3 | 5.3 | −1.0 |
| Health and Human Services | 116.4 | 107.4 | −9.0 |
| Interior | 2.4 | 2.6 | +0.2 |
| Justice | 2.6 | 2.9 | +0.3 |
| Labor | 43.7 | 66.7 | +23 |
| State | 0.4 | 0.4 | −0.1 |
| Treasury | 91.9 | 91.1 | −0.8 |
| Social Security Administration | 14.2 | 13.8 | −0.4 |
| Education | 93.5 | 87.2 | −6.3 |
| Energy | 18.9 | 19.4 | +0.5 |
| Environmental Protection Agency | 4.3 | 6.4 | +2.1 |
| Transportation | 31.5 | 31.9 | +0.5 |
| General Services Administration | 2.6 | 3.1 | +0.5 |
| Homeland Security | 2.0 | 1.3 | −0.7 |
| Housing and Urban Development | 8.3 | 11.0 | +2.7 |
| All other | 10.2 | 9.0 | −1.1 |
| **Total** | **473.5** | **494.0** | **+20.4** |

*Source*: Data from US Congressional Budget Office (2012).

**Table 4.3** Total ARRA funds for education (in billions)

| Program | Total allocated |
|---|---|
| State Fiscal Stabilization Fund | 48.6 |
| •Education State Grants | 39.8 |
| •Government Services Grants | 8.8 |
| Pell Grants | 17.1 |
| Special Education | 12.2 |
| •IDEA State Grants | 11.7 |
| •IDEA Infants and Family Grants | 0.5 |
| •IDEA Pre-School Grants | 0.4 |
| Title 1 Education for the Disadvantaged | 10.0 |
| Race to the Top and Investing in Education | 5.0 |
| School Improvement Grants | 3.0 |
| Rehabilitation Services and Disability Research | 0.54 |
| Educational Technology Grants | 0.65 |
| State Longitudinal Data Systems Grants | 0.2 |
| Work Study | 0.2 |
| Teacher Incentive Fund | 0.2 |
| Teacher Quality Enhancement | 0.1 |
| Impact Aid | 0.1 |
| McKinney Vento Homeless Education Grants | 0.07 |
| Student Aid Administration | 0.06 |
| **Total** | **98.2** |

*Source*: Data from US Department of Education (2009).

## Reforming US Education

Taken as a whole, the Obama administration entered office on a mandate of neo-Keynesian government intervention to resolve a wide range of socioeconomic challenges facing the United States. Indeed, since taking office, the Obama administration has justified its educational reform policies in terms of the need to develop competitive human capital:

> For we know that economic progress and educational achievement have always gone hand in hand in America...The source of America's prosperity has never been merely how ably we accumulate wealth, but how well we educate our people. This has never been more true than it is today. In a 21st-century world where jobs can be

shipped wherever there's an Internet connection...where your best job qualification is not what you do, but what you know—education is no longer just a pathway to opportunity and success, it's a prerequisite for success. (Obama, 2009, pp. 5–6)

Mounting concern about the future of the US economy has translated into education policies that emphasize command-and-control management models that build on superficial reforms of industrial era education. Indeed, a large and a growing number of interest groups including policymakers, business leaders, and educators have become highly focused on educational reform in order to improve human capital performance. Advancing on the rationale that national educational standards will improve academic performance, Secretary of Education Arne Duncan (2009) has focused on the need for a set of "common, career-ready internationally benchmarked standards" to drive economic competitiveness. Coordinated by the National Governors Association (NGA) and the Council of Chief State School Officers (CCSSO), the Common Core State Standards Initiative (CCSSI) defines college and career readiness as the ability "to succeed in entry-level, credit-bearing academic college courses and in workforce-training programs."

Rather than a specific curriculum, CCSSI is viewed as a shared framework for interpreting common goals and expectations about K-12 schooling, while at the same time leaving teachers to construct lesson plans and tailor instruction. Opponents of CCSSI, however, argue that a federally driven education system undermines the experimental capacity built into the US education system (Zhao, 2009, 2012b). Mitigating both sides is the fact that CCSSI has been institutionalized at the state level rather than at the federal level. Allowing for some customization, for example, CCSSI has a provision in the voluntary adoption guidelines that permits states to supplement up to 15 percent of the common core standards with state-level standards. Building on this framework, the Obama administration has sought to increase the percentage of US college graduates (defined as either two- or four-year degrees) from 39 percent to 60 percent of the population by 2020.

Part of the problem with the application of CCSSI, however, is that it has largely reinforced neoliberal social policies. Notwithstanding the fact the Obama administration has emphasized the need to move beyond neoliberalism (Peters, 2012), this has not translated into changes in US education policy. The main problem is that federal education policies have done little to transform market-based assumptions about factory-driven schooling.

Building on the policies of the Bush administration, for example, President Obama's education policies have focused on the expansion of charter schools and the use of performance-based compensation for shaping teacher compliance.

At the center of the president's K-12 education reform agenda, for example, is the "Race to the Top" (RTTT) grants competition. Using stimulus funding as a lever for social reform, the administration has attempted to steer educational reform through funding provisions that attempt to nationalize the US education system. More to the point, stimulus funding has been used by the Obama administration to craft a political agenda designed to compel needy states to follow federally mandated standards. As McDonnell & Weatherford (2011, p. 315) point out, this approach to educational reform has had three distinct strengths but also one significant weakness.

Strengths:

- A large discretionary funding source with little Congressional scrutiny over how it intended to use the funds.
- Avoidance of the kind of "agenda jamming" that had derailed Bill Clinton's first-year initiatives.
- Ability to frame the national discussion around education reform without being constrained by negotiations over the details of specific legislation.

Weakness:

- A lack of support "on the ground."

Perhaps the major weakness of RTTT has been its "top-down" application. Although the economic stimulus has provided a pretext for significant investments in educational reform, the pace at which these reforms have been implemented may have in fact set in motion a whole new set of problems.

By attaching conditions to receipt of stimulus funds, the Obama administration has implemented significant national educational reform without mobilizing local support among the nation's teachers. Lacking the endogenous support of teachers and their broader support communities, it is hard to imagine that stimulus-driven educational reforms will bear fruit. As "with many past education reforms, the Obama administration has emphasized the central role of teachers—how they are recruited, trained, evaluated, and compensated. In doing so, it faces a classic dilemma: the group the administration has identified as a central part of the problem is the one on whom it must depend to solve that problem" (McDonnell & Weatherford, 2011, p. 316). It remains to be seen whether President Obama's educational reforms will have impact over the long term.

## A Blueprint for Reform: The Reauthorization of the Elementary and Secondary Education Act

Building on the adoption of "college and career-ready" standards, *A Blueprint for Reform* (BFR) (US Department of Education, 2010a) represents the Obama administration's official plan to reform the Elementary and Secondary Education Act (ESEA). In fact, BFR is the primary federal legislation governing K-12 public education in the United States. Originally introduced as a federal statute in 1965 by President Johnson, ESEA explicitly forbids the establishment of a national curriculum, focusing instead on state-administered, federally funded programs for primary and secondary education. Taken as a whole, BFR emphasizes four areas:

- improvement of teacher/principal effectiveness;
- provision of tools and information to families that will help them evaluate their children's schools;
- implementation of college-and-career-ready standards; and
- provision of intensive support and effective interventions that will help improve student learning and achievement in America's lowest-performing schools.

Intentionally broad, the plan's stated goal is to increase local control and provide necessary federal support. This includes Title I programs (a provision of ESEA), which are the primary funding source for lower-income children and students.

In truth, BFR is a response to criticism of the No Child Left Behind Act (NCLB) introduced by the Bush administration. Amended and reauthorized in 2002 by President Bush, NCLB overlaps Title I funding[3] which is given to schools where at least 35 percent of children come from low-income families or to schools where 35 percent of the student population is low-income (which includes more than 50% of all public schools). Criticism of NCLB's punitive approach to educational reform, however, has overshadowed BFR. In response to this criticism, BFR states:

> Throughout this proposal, we have sought to redefine the federal role in education: shifting from a focus merely on compliance to allowing state and local innovation to flourish, rewarding success, and fostering supportive and collaborative relationships with states, districts, and nonprofit partners. There are several cross-cutting changes we are proposing in order to allow local innovations to lead the way and to support the development, identification, and scaling-up of strategies that are working. (p. 39)

To this end, new systems of evaluation are introduced to capture more in-depth assessments of student achievement. Specific revisions to NCLB include funding for states to develop a broader range of assessments to evaluate advanced academic skills, including students' abilities to conduct research, use technology, engage in scientific investigation, solve problems, and communicate effectively. Improvement measures also include expanded assessment for English language learners, minorities, and students with special needs. To its credit, BFR leaves room for varied intervention models, with the key idea being that the federal government does not mandate a specific model. At the same time, if a school does not improve sufficiently, the state can close or "restart" the school as a charter school.

Building on NCLB, BFR supports "standards-based education reform" rooted in the assumption that high standards and measurable goals boost performance outcomes. This framework includes:

(1) rigorous college and career-ready standards;
(2) rigorous and fair accountability and support at every level;
(3) measuring and supporting schools, districts, and states;

(4) building capacity and support and every level; and
(5) fostering comparability and equity.

Federal grants are targeted at supporting standards and assessments developed at the state level, including formula grants for high-poverty districts. States have the option of working with four-year public universities or working with other states to establish common standards (particularly in math and English). These reforms include developing the necessary data-gathering systems to measure performance and "reward success." However, data must be made publicly available and include measurements such as graduation rates, college enrollment rates, and disaggregated based on race, gender, ethnicity, disability, etc. States and districts are encouraged to reward successful schools and reach performance targets. To ensure equity, districts are expected to measure and balance resources between high-poverty and low-poverty schools. In turn, states receive funds to design programs using one of four turnaround models for low performing "Challenge schools." These four models are developmental in approach:

1. Transformation model: Replace the principal, strengthen staffing, implement a research-based instructional program, provide extended learning time, and implement new governance and flexibility.
2. Turnaround model: Replace the principal and rehire no more than 50 percent of the school staff, implement a research-based instructional program, provide extended learning time, and implement new governance structure.
3. Restart model: Convert or close and reopen the school under the management of an effective charter operator, charter management organization, or education management organization.
4. School closure model: Close the school and enroll students who attended it in other, higher-performing schools in the district.

## Great Teachers and Great Leaders

With a particular focus on measuring teacher and principal "effectiveness," BFR emphasizes statewide assessment indicators in conjunction with state-level data systems and district-level evaluation systems that

> (i) meaningfully differentiate teachers and principals by effectiveness across at least three performance levels; (ii) are consistent with their state's definitions of effective and highly effective teacher and principal; (iii) provide meaningful feedback to teachers and principals to improve their practice and inform professional development; and (iv) are developed in collaboration with teachers, principals, and other education stakeholders. (p. 15)

Building on published "report cards" and corresponding to reward systems used in the private sector, BFR emphasizes "differentiated compensation and career advancement opportunities" in order to incent "educators who are effective in increasing student academic achievement, who take on additional roles and responsibilities in their schools, and who teach in high-need schools, subjects, areas, and fields" (p. 16).

## Meeting the Needs of English Learners and Other Diverse Learners

BFR also includes grant support for the evaluation of programs serving special populations including English language learners, students with disabilities, Native American students, homeless students, the children of migrant workers, and neglected or delinquent students. Specific examples include (p. 19):

- Improving programs for English Learners and encouraging innovative programs and practices to support English Learners' success and build the knowledge base about what works.
- Maintaining and strengthening formula grant programs for Native American students, homeless students, migrant students, and neglected or delinquent students; as well as for districts that are in rural areas or that are affected by federal property and activities.
- Meeting the needs of students with disabilities throughout ESEA and through the Individuals with Disabilities Education Act.

## A Complete Education

Additionally, competitive grants to states are provided in support of literacy and STEM subjects that build on state standards, including subgrants to high-needs districts. As an amendment to NCLB, partial emphasis is placed on "arts, foreign languages, history and civics, financial literacy, environmental education, and other subjects" (p. 28). Priority is focused on states that develop common standards, use technology to address learning challenges, consider universal design for learning principles, and align coursework with colleges and universities (including Advanced Placement and International Baccalaureate programs). Additional grant funding is set aside for innovative application of educational technology and digital media (including innovation grants to nonprofits).

## Successful, Safe, and Healthy Students

Responding to concerns about the need for community engagement, BFR emphasizes an educational *continuum* (from birth though career) that supports "effective community services, strong family supports, and comprehensive education reforms...in high-need communities" (p. 32). Priority is placed on states, school districts, and nonprofit organizations that develop programs for Challenge schools that may redesign and expand the school schedule, including supports for nonprofits and community-based organizations. To ensure "school safety," grantees are required to "develop and implement a state- or district-wide school climate needs assessment to evaluate school engagement, school safety (addressing drug, alcohol, and violence issues), and school environment, and publicly report this information" (p. 33).

## Fostering Innovation and Excellence

Modeled after the Race to the Top program authorized by ARRA, BFR leverages competitive funding against state-directed comprehensive reforms in standards and assessment. States and school districts are required to develop and implement comprehensive plans to improve student outcomes as measured by annual performance targets. Building on ARRA's i3 (Investing in Innovation) program, additional competitive grants are provided to support evidence-based practice linked to independent evaluation. Perhaps, most controversially, BFR promotes "public school choice" by providing competitive grant funding to charter schools.

## Discussion: The Problem with A Blueprint for Reform

The truth is that BFR builds on a long tradition of federal educational reform in the United States. In fact, there have been several Presidential commissions examining educational reform in the United States over the last century. These include the Truman Report (1947), the Committee on Education Beyond the High School (1956), the Task Force on Education (1960), the National Commission on Excellence in Education (which produced A Nation at Risk) (1983), and the Commission on the Future of Higher Education (2006). Despite an explicit focus on "excellence for all," the implicit focus of US federal education policy has long been education as a foundation to economic growth.

Following on from President Bush, the Obama administration has used government-led investments in education to extend NCLB legislation as part of a broader mandate of nationalizing educational reform. Building on a growing global focus on standards-based reform, BFR serves as an instrument for "rationalizing" the US education system. The overriding assumption is that the development of rigorous academic standards linked to clear and measurable assessments will lead to high-quality curricular and pedagogical practices. Reinforcing this assumption is an economic rationale that directly links high-quality education and student achievement to economic performance. Much as NCLB, BFR relies on standardized testing to measure improvement. In fact, failure to improve academic performance can trigger faculty termination and/or the transformation of public schools into semi-privatized charter schools.

The main goal of BFR is to promote academic consistency across states through a federalized accountability system. Although cosmetic changes in language are introduced—"Teacher Quality" becomes

"Teacher Effectiveness," the underlying principles of NCLB remain the same. BFR directs states to implement high-quality statewide assessments that align with newly developed state standards, including yearly testing in reading and math from grades three through eight. Moreover, where NCLB imposes no requirements on content or standards developed by states, BFR requires states to develop and adopt state standards in English and mathematics. While states may choose to retain their current standards or work together and collaboratively develop new common standards that ideally mirror the National Governor's Association Common Core Standards. Only those states that have implemented assessment based on common state standards by 2015 receive formula funds.

Notwithstanding its many strengths, one of the key weaknesses of BFR is a palpable disdain for the professional capacities of public teachers in the United States. This is seen, for example, in the use of incentivization schemes that emphasize merit pay as a means to steer teacher performance. Kumashiro (2012, p. 9) notes that merit pay represents a "form of positive reinforcement," with the underlying supposition that teachers can be persuaded to work harder through behavioral rewards. The truth is that many of the problems associated with contemporary US education—including the achievement gap—are unfairly mapped onto teachers. As critical scholars note, many of the acute tensions facing US schools today are rooted in a complex history of social and political inequity. Recent expansion in educational access due to civil rights legislation has meant that public education has become a platform for class-based social struggle (Spring, 2008; Lipman, 2009; Kumashiro, 2012).

Despite a historic legacy of discrimination based around racial segregation, radical funding inequity, and meager investments in quality education, students from working-class and poor families continue to remain subject to rigid and punitive disciplinary regimes As Saltman (2010a) notes:

> The key point here is that standardization (as typified by standardized testing, the regressive linkage of school funding to test scores, value added assessment, etc.) is being deployed differently in working-class and poor public schools as opposed to in professional-class public schools. It is not only that pedagogical and curricular matters are being reformed differently, but that the professional-class schools

continue to receive public investment while the schools of working class and poor students in both urban and rural areas are being transformed into a new kind of commodified lower tier through privatization. (p. 390)

In Garrison's (2012) terms, the testing regime itself reflects a misguided form of class structure that fuses technocratic business systems to caste-based social structures. Under this system, "schools assume the task of standardizing human capital as a commodity suitable for ready exchange that fits docilely into the existing sociopolitical-economic order rather than democratic individuals charged with challenging and changing the status quo" (p. 371). In truth, the history of inequity in the United States has created a structural legacy that now uses schools as scapegoats for class- and race-based oppression.

Indeed, much of the focus on testing in the United States reflects the interests of private sector reform groups that have directly challenged teacher unions, school administrators, and local school boards so that decision making is no longer primarily determined by school leaders and elected officials who are governing schools and making policy decision but rather, by mega-philanthropies and corporations. According to Kumashiro (2012, p. 7),

> the megaphilanthropies, like the Gates and Broad foundations, are exerting unprecedented influence over school reform. Although philanthropic funding continues to constitute only a small percentage of school funding, its influence is disproportionately large as it engages a corporate-based strategy to leverage wealth, not unlike the venture capitalists (Saltman, 2010b; Scott, 2009). This is where the term "venture philanthropies" comes from. Venture capitalists are those who leverage their wealth to make more money, and similarly, venture philanthropies are leveraging their wealth to influence policy. Primarily, these philanthropies target urban areas with the intention of piloting certain types of reforms eventually to scale up nationwide, which is why we see so much Gates and Broad funding coming into cities like Chicago (Lipman, 2011). Corporations also exert increasing influence over school reform. One example is Pearson, which dominates not only the testing market but also the test-preparation market, and is profiting enormously from funding initiatives like Race to the Top that require substantial outsourcing.

Consequently, it is among the most influential educational lobbyists right now.

To put this in perspective, consider that between 2005 and 2009, the Gates Foundation spent $78 million on advocacy and funded the groups that wrote, evaluated, and promoted the Common Core Standards, the centerpiece of President Obama's educational policy reforms (Ravitch, 2011, p. 277). Indeed, after decades of school reforms designed around neoliberal social policies, numerous studies have shown very high percentages of students struggling academically or leaving the education system altogether (Barton, 2005; Friedlaender and Darling-Hammond, 2007). Citing a recent nine-year study, Ravitch (2011, p. 282) notes:

> In 2011, the National Research Council of the National Academies of Science, our nation's most prestigious research organization, released a nine-year study called "Incentives and Test-based Accountability." A seventeen-member panel of social scientists, including some of the foremost experts in the world, assessed the value of tying test scores to incentives: that is, to carrots and sticks, rewards and punishments. The panel concluded that test-based accountability led to score inflation, to gaming the system, and to behaviors that undermined the value of the scores. They also reviewed the evidence and found that test-based incentives have a decidedly meager track record in boosting student achievement... When students practice the test content day after day, they learn to take the test, but the scores may not truly indicate their skills or knowledge. We have adopted a national strategy designed to raise test scores without necessarily improving the quality of education.

In response to the goals of BFR, many scholars argue that testing is the wrong vehicle for improving academic performance. Scholars collaborating with the National Education Policy Center (NEPC), for example, found that policies underlying BFR simply lacked an independent research base (Mathis and Welner, 2010). Despite the fact that BFR specifically argues for the need to base policymaking on the strength of empirical research (p. 41), reviewers of the document and its summaries[4] (US Department of Education, 2010b) found them to be largely partisan documents. In fact, according to Mathis and Welner (2010), this includes a "general neglect of peer-reviewed research and an over-reliance on information gathered from special interest groups, think tanks, government documents, and media reports" (p. 5). Put another way, BFR is better described as a strategy document than a research-based policy document.

Indeed, the most damning criticism of BFR is that it simply lacks the evidentiary basis upon which to form an empirical critique. Vital omissions include a lack of specific detail around: (1) a justification for or explanation of the accountability system used to evaluate schools (the linchpin of the proposal); (2) the intervention models used to address low-scoring schools; (3) the research evidence demonstrating the value of competitive grants and/or charter schools for leveraging quality improvement (versus further increasing financial inequity between high-performing and low-performing schools). As Mathis and Welner (2010, p. 6) conclude:

> Research should play a role in the formulation of policy. But it must be used to enlighten our discussions and not as selective, *post hoc* justification for pre-determined ideological positions. For many of the nation's educational problems, such as those catalogued in the *Blueprint*, there is a well-developed, informative, scientifically valid and independently established body of research. For those areas where our knowledge base is not yet mature, the wisest approach would be to actively seek new knowledge through pilot programs before mandating unproven solutions as national policies.
>
> If our goal is a more educated citizenry, our policies must be based on our best knowledge and experience. Otherwise, we risk weakening our educational system as well as our civic, economic, and social institutions. Sadly, it appears that the Obama administration is poised to continue the political misuse of research... The federal government can contribute to improving our schools most effectively when policymakers in the Department of Education seek and embrace research-based solutions—even when the research contradicts the politics or prevailing ideologies of the day.

As these scholars point out, in addition to the very weak research base supporting BFR, the major problem with President Obama's educational reform plan is its sweeping ideological assumptions. Building on the testing regime at the core of NCLB and an aggressive focus on charter schools, President Obama has attempted to federalize US education without the proper investment in public policy research.

This is a significant problem because it speaks to larger challenges confronting US public policy as a whole.

## Transforming American Education: Learning Powered by Technology

In the same year as *Blueprint for Reform*, Secretary of Education Arne Duncan released the final version of the administration's National Educational Technology Plan (US Department of Education, 2010c), a five-year action plan authored by a Technical Working Group (TWG) focused on educational technology. Presented to the US Congress by the Department of Education, the National Educational Technology Plan (NETP) represents the thinking of many of the leading scholars and practitioners on educational reform in the United States. Less a plan for implementing educational technology and more a plan for redesigning the US education system, NETP offers a broad array of suggestions for transforming education. At its core, "Transforming American Education: Learning Powered by Technology" (US Department of Education, 2010c) encourages structural changes to classroom education through the use of digital technologies. As the opening to the Executive Summary reads,

> Education is the key to America's economic growth and prosperity and to our ability to compete in the global economy. It is the path to good jobs and higher earning power for Americans. It is necessary for our democracy to work. It fosters the cross-border, crosscultural collaboration required to solve the most challenging problems of our time. (p. 7)

Seeking to leverage technology to "revolutionize" education, NETP is intended as a blueprint for next generation education. As the authors observe, "technology-based learning and assessment systems will be pivotal in improving student learning and generating data that can be used to continuously improve the education system at all levels" (p. 7). Against the backdrop of cost and revenue concerns, the report outlines several goals for reforming education across five areas: (1) learning, (2) assessment, (3) teaching, (4) infrastructure, and (5) productivity.

## Learning: Engage and Empower

Emphasizing personalized learning, NETP suggests that the "limitless, borderless, and instantaneous" nature of digital media now challenges education to develop engaging multimedia rich learning environments that support self-directed learning and twenty-first-century competencies. This includes the use of Web tools (blogs, wikis, social networks) and data and visualization tools to scaffold student experiences with "real-world" problems.

## Assessment: Measure What Matters

The report highlights the need for new forms of formative and summative assessment that might both diagnose and monitor student learning, as well as provide feedback on the education system as a whole. Underlining the need to adopt Common Core Standards, the report suggests that data-driven systems can improve learning outcomes and provide continuous feedback to students, educators, parents, and administrators.

## Teaching: Prepare and Connect

The plan also calls for teacher capacity building in STEM competencies and team-based teaching (or connected teaching) through professional communities of practice. Educators are viewed as critical to reforming education provided they are properly trained, rewarded, and supported by ubiquitous access to resources, data, and analytical tools. The systemic lack of technology literacy across the field of education (teachers, researchers, and policymakers), for example, is seen as a significant challenge.

## Infrastructure: Access and Enable

Underlying all five goals of NETP is technology as an enabling (cyber) infrastructure for education. This includes both institutional infrastructure (people, processes, learning resources, policies, and models for improvement) and technical infrastructure (broadband connectivity, networks, servers, software, and management systems). NETP suggests that technology is now at an inflection point in which cloud computing and OER could transform education from a system of "rigid information transfer" into an "always on" network connecting data, learning communities, and multimedia resources. As the plan observes, part of the challenge is creating interoperability standards for content and student-learning data to improve decision making at all levels of the system.

Productivity: Redesign and Transform

Building on the need for infrastructure and taking its lead from the private sector, NETP advocates fundamental structural changes to education around data management and continuous improvement. This includes managing and monitoring financial performance data, integrating diverse data systems, and adopting common cost-accounting standards to benchmark and analyze costs over time. As the authors point out, K-12 education spending per student has increased by more than 70 percent over the last 30 years without a commensurate improvement in outcomes. The plan suggests rethinking basic assumptions including restructuring schooling by competence (rather than age or "seat time"), introducing flexible scheduling (around student needs) particularly through online education, and utilizing "smart" systems.

## Discussion: Interpreting NETP

Of the three policy documents examined here, NETP offers perhaps the most compelling vision for transforming US education in light of the needs of a postindustrial society. Building on an economic development rationale, NETP focuses on aligning the use of digital technologies in schools with the broader applications of technology in the workplace. Accordingly, education is now an urgent priority driven by the need for a more highly educated workforce with particular STEM competencies and skills. Taken as a whole, NETP is comprehensive in its recommendations for structural changes to schooling. The main deficits of NETP, however, are its underappreciation of the growing need to make education highly personalized (relative to the Creative Economy) and networked (relative to the Network Economy). While the plan is effective at laying out an extensive framework (across learning, assessment, teaching, infrastructure, and productivity) for technology-mediated education, its strengths mostly lie in pointing to the need for developing a new and advanced technological infrastructure supporting educational transformation (especially teaching and assessment). Perhaps, more importantly, NETP points to the need for developing incentives for solving the "grand challenge problems" facing education.[5]

Indeed, the key strength of NETP is a focus on the need to resolve pervasive challenges facing postindustrial society. As the document concludes, perhaps the ultimate grand challenge facing us today is education itself:

> Today, we have examples of systems that can recommend learning resources a person might like, learning materials with embedded tutoring functions, software that can provide UDL supports for any technology-based learning materials, and learning management systems that move individuals through sets of learning materials and keep track of their progress and activity. What we do not have is an integrated system that can perform all these functions dynamically while optimizing engagement and learning for all learners. Such an integrated system is essential for implementing the individualized, differentiated, and personalized learning called for in this plan. (p. 78)

This point would be much stronger, however, if it were more directly linked to creativity and innovation, a point I will return to in chapter 6.

In fact, critics of NETP argue that the plan does not go far enough. Horn & Mackey (2011), for example, suggest that the plan is simply too iterative and lacks a strategy for disruptive innovation. Where the plan's authors suggest that disruptive innovations are more likely to come from the "edge" than the "core"— with formal education only being one node in an emerging learning ecology (Atkins et al., 2011), critics respond that this fails to address the limitations within education itself. Waks (2011), for example, argues that NETP lacks the kind of radical ideas on transformation that are now commonplace outside of the education system. As he points out, the chief distinction to be made in evaluating NETP is between centralized and distributed control models:

> [Transforming American Education] has two cardinal features: (a) strengthening the dominance of SOC [standard subject matter,

analyzed into goals, objectives, and competencies] in curriculum, teaching, assessment through a pervasive system of measurements and controls, and (b) diversifying learning environments and methods for conveying SOC and connecting teachers for collaboration and exchange in the delivery of SOC. This adds up to greater control over learning by the central, financially dependent state and local educational agencies, and stakeholder clients. (Waks, 2011, p. 5)

The main problem, in other words, is that NETP continues the command-and-control model for micromanaging education, rather than capitalizing on the network affordances of technology. Put differently, while it seeks to replace the limitations of the factory school, NETP manages instead to construct a "flexitronic" model of schooling (Waks, 2011) that leaves the underlying structure of the factory school unchanged.

## Conclusion

Analysis of public policy documents authored by the Obama administration suggests that education policies are ill-suited to the challenges facing US education today. Indeed, the central problem with contemporary education reform policies is that they are simply outmoded. Locked into the factory logics of the industrial age, the Obama administration has made insufficient effort to analyze the broad technological transformation that is remaking US society and economy. Additionally, the lack of credible educational research supporting federal education policies has produced flawed policy proposals. The truth is that each feature of factory schooling has been fine-tuned to fit an older industrial social order that is now vanishing (Waks, 2013). It is for this reason that any reform of US education will require a systemic shift that builds on a new paradigm of learning linked to a global knowledge economy.

The rise of competitive international benchmarking systems like PISA and TIMSS (Trends in International Mathematics and Science Study) reflect an expanding global competition between national economies based around a capacity for skilled labor and national systems of innovation. This globalization of competition is driving a convergence of policies and strategies that key educational reform to the assessment and ranking of educational performance (Rizvi and Lingard, 2010). The consequence of this policy shift is that a large and growing industry has evolved around the use of standardized testing to measure and assess learning. In the United States, this testing regime is often justified on the grounds that standardized testing can assist in "closing the achievement gap" between middle-class and working-class students. This is despite the fact that research has clearly shown that this achievement gap is rooted in an extensive history of discrimination, segregation, and inequitable funding (Ladson-Billings, 2006; Kumashiro, 2012). Indeed, under neoliberal social policies, the achievement gap has widened substantially with some "school districts spending more than four times as much per student as neighboring districts" (Kumashiro, 2012, p. 7).

Notwithstanding the obvious importance of education as a means for national economic development, there remain open questions about the long-term effectiveness of the reform strategies now applied in US education policy. Critical educationalists, for example, argue that raising the achievement scores of disadvantaged students in order to enroll more students in higher education will not solve the growing challenges facing the US economy. As Garrison (2012) notes, the problem today is that the testing regime itself checks the very "development of genuine individuality by keying social success toward a relatively small array of attributes approved by the aristocratic classes and away from those attributes that might threaten existing power structures by releasing unique potential" (p. 375). Indeed, it is my view that the education system itself needs to be fundamentally reimagined. Rather than incrementally improving basic academic skills, the solution to educational reform is rooted in fundamentally rethinking the purpose of schools.

In chapter 5, I point to the need to move beyond economic philosophies that anchor schooling to educating factory workers for a mass society. More specifically, I speculate on the potential of new forms of social and economic investment that might move human development beyond the constraints imposed by neoliberal social policy. Using interviews with scholars and policymakers focused on KE, I develop an interpretative account of the kinds of changes that I believe are needed in US education. As these interviews make clear, systems of education are now facing an evolutionary phase shift that will inevitably move schooling beyond the industrial era.

## Chapter 5

# The Knowledge Economy in Dialogue

### Implications for US Educational Reform

Throughout this book I have argued that educational reform today is undermined by a superficial reading of the broad social and technological changes that are now remaking postindustrial societies. Despite narrow and often monolithic readings of KE, there remain open questions about the kind of education that will best serve students in the twenty-first century. Indeed, rather than simply one "knowledge economy," there are in fact many conflicting paradigms of KE that are together producing significant ambiguity in the design of educational reform.

Perhaps the central challenge facing knowledge-based economies today is that the structures underlying the production, preservation, and transmission of knowledge are changing (McNeely and Wolverton, 2008). As computerization enables deep structural changes in work and learning, it is simultaneously making many forms of labor redundant. In this chapter, I present interview research and findings with a particular interest in advancing a new policy framework for reconstructing US educational reform. Beyond the era of factory production, students are now under pressure to demonstrate a wide range of competencies linked to knowledge-based innovation (Zhao, 2012b). In truth, technology is shaping new institutional potentials and coalescing around entirely new formations of network-driven production and consumption.

Notwithstanding the importance of "skills development" in the context of STEM disciplines, there is in fact a broad range of sociotechnical capacities needed for advancing KE. Chief among these is the creative application of new knowledge through entrepreneurship and innovation. As technologies "like robotics, numerically controlled machines, computerized inventory control, and automatic transcription" substitute for routine tasks, new generations of Americans are now expected to become increasingly entrepreneurial (Brynjolfsson and McAfee, 2011, p. 41). Building on this understanding, I argue that a key theme linking all discourses of KE is the importance of creativity and innovation in the broad transformation of industrial civilization.

## The Knowledge Economy in Dialogue

In this chapter, I reflect on the interview research supporting this book. Building on interviews with scholars, researchers, and policymakers whose work overlaps learning in the context of KE, I offer tentative proposals for reforming US education. Experts interviewed for this research include:

1. Richard Florida, director of the Martin Prosperity Institute at the University of Toronto, and leading proponent on the Creative Economy.
2. Michel Bauwens, founder of the Foundation for Peer-to-Peer Alternatives, and noted expert on the Network Economy.
3. Sam Pitroda, former Chairman of India's National Knowledge Commission (2005–2009), advisor to the prime minister of India, and global expert on technology policy and educational reform.
4. Cathy Davidson, a distinguished scholar of the history of technology, noted expert on digital media and learning, and recently appointed member of the National Humanities Council by President Obama.
5. Donald Brinkman, program manager at Microsoft Research in digital humanities, digital heritage, and games for learning, and former program manager with the Education Products Group.

Table 5.1 Four paradigms of the Knowledge Economy

| | Paradigm 1 | Paradigm 2 | Paradigm 3 | Paradigm 4 |
|---|---|---|---|---|
| **Key focus** | Neoliberal Knowledge Economy<br>Human capital | Network Economy<br>Network commons | Creative Economy<br>Intellectual capital | Green Economy<br>Green innovation |
| **Key actor** | Knowledge worker | Peer producer (Produser) | Creative class | Green jobs |
| **Learning/Training focus** | STEM skills | Collaboration (peer production) | Innovation/Entrepreneurship | Clean technologies |
| **Educational disciplines** | Business Management, Engineering, Science and Technology, Math/Statistics | Computer and Information Sciences | Communication, Architecture, Art, Design and Media, Computer Science | Natural Science, Environmental Science, Engineering, Computer Science |
| **Key themes** | Innovation, R&D, intellectual property | Mass collaboration, peer production, open source technologies | Human ingenuity, intellectual property | Clean technologies, innovation, sustainability |
| **Key industries** | Engineering, Biotechnology, IT, Management, Finance | Social media, open science, open hardware, crowdsourcing | Design, Publishing, Film, Arts, Architecture, Software | Wind, Solar, Biomass, Smart Grid, Software |

6. Tony Wagner, Innovation Education Fellow at the Technology & Entrepreneurship Center at Harvard University and the founder and codirector of the Change Leadership Group at the Harvard Graduate School of Education.
7. Tony Seba, lecturer in entrepreneurship and clean energy at Stanford University, a noted Silicon Valley expert on the Green Economy, and a member of the advisory board of the Stanford Society for Entrepreneurship in Latin America.

As this book has attempted to demonstrate, one of the underlying problems facing educational reform today is that there is no single vision or definition of KE through which to rethink US education policy. In fact, new developments in an overlapping and expanding literature on economics, sociology, and management studies suggest that definitions of KE continue to proliferate. What we do know is that rather than framing educational reform in terms of the needs of a mass industrial economy, educational policies must now drive toward the needs of a global knowledge economy. Part of the problem, however, is that there is no consensus on what redesigning education for a global knowledge economy amounts to. Looking at the four paradigms outlined above (table 5.1), for example, we find several distinctive and conflicting discourses on KE.

In the sections that follow, I present a critical analysis of US educational reform that builds on research interviews conducted for this book. I begin with a discussion on human capital formation and the Neoliberal Knowledge Economy (Paradigm 1), and continue with discussions on peer production and the Network Economy (Paradigm 2), creative practice and the Creative Economy (Paradigm 3), and green innovation and the Green Economy (Paradigm 4). Lastly, I consider the implications of each paradigm for shaping US education policy.

## Paradigm 1: Human Capital Formation and the Neoliberal Knowledge Economy

Moving beyond models of education that merely reinforce basic schooling, many advocates of KE argue that STEM competencies are now fundamental to stimulating growth within postindustrial societies. Underlying this view of educational reform is the notion that developing advanced human capital is the key to driving innovation. As Sam Pitroda, key advisor to the prime minister of India suggests, human capital development is now seen as critical to the future success of emerging economies.

Pitroda:

> Policymakers believe that we need to focus on really improving [the] quality of people. See when I look at the global scenario today I find that we have spent billions and billions in improving the quality of products but we have not spent time and money to create people... So we are not really focused on creating people... [A]t the end of the day we believe you need young people to focus on discipline, analytical ability, creativity, respect for the other viewpoint, ethics, globalization, and a multidisciplinary approach to everything.

As chairman of India's National Innovation Council, Pitroda argues that schools in the twenty-first century are foundational to leveraging innovation. He points to the daunting challenges facing India's development and the country's critical need for skilled labor.

Pitroda:

> We need to create 20 million new jobs year after year, how do we do that without focusing on knowledge? So we need to improve education, knowledge institutions and... we need *development*. Everything is happening in India but perhaps not happening fast enough. We're not building roads fast enough; we're not improving power requirements fast enough. For all of these we really need knowledge to drive these initiatives.
>
> So [the] Knowledge Commission has eight members, we meet once every couple of months for two or three days and we look at essentially five aspects of knowledge. Access to knowledge, knowledge concepts, knowledge creation, knowledge applications and knowledge production.... Then we look at all knowledge concepts which relate to education, school education, work education, distance learning, open education, university education, teacher training. We also look at things like how do we get more of our kids to go into math and science. How do we get more kids to go through PhD programs? Then we look at [the] creation of knowledge, who creates knowledge, how knowledge is created.

> Essentially we focus on innovations, entrepreneurship, patents, copyright, trademarks, and all that. Then we look at application of knowledge in agriculture, health, small- and medium-scale industries, and traditional knowledge. We have [a] large amount of traditional knowledge that we need to digitize, computerize, organize, sort it out whether it has to do with music, art, herbal medicines, yoga, you know, we just finished documenting a million manuscripts into digital format. These are manuscripts written 1500 years ago on banana leaves, for example. You can get all of these on the Web today. Then finally we look at e-governance to focus on the role of knowledge in improving governments, at [the] federal level, at [the] state level and at [the] district level. So some total, we look at about 30 different subjects in knowledge. We decided to set up a knowledge commission and not a commission on education, not a commission on IT, nor on science and technology. Rather than the vertical slice, we decided to look at the horizontal slice.

Much as India, US educational reform is now largely shaped by related concerns about the need for maximizing human capital formation. The policy approach taken by the Obama administration, for example, has been a strong focus on "nationalizing" the US education system in order to standardize access to quality schooling. This is a common worry in the United States where concern about human capital formation directly focused on rising inequality. Tony Seba, a noted Silicon Valley entrepreneur and university educator, argues that unequal access to quality education is the central problem facing US economy and society.

Seba:

> Education should be a lifetime pursuit now. The half-life of knowledge or the half-life of skills is getting shorter and shorter...[and] I think inequality of access to education is the biggest challenge facing the US today. It's not a question of people or technology or money; it's inequality of access to education. You know, the top institutions are lavishly financed and well managed, but pretty much the rest are left to their own devices...and they just can't compete. Most education at the high school and middle school level is local. And local funding and local management just cannot compete with the quality of the top 1 percent or so. And local education means that education is overly politicized. You have politicians and lobbyists setting not just educational goals, but actually writing the content in textbooks and classrooms...This is not just dangerous; this is ignorant.

Seba echoes the view that education in the United States should be much more centralized in order to improve upon gaps in quality. In his view, a more coherent national education system is critical to minimizing inequality.

Seba:

> We definitely need a more *national* educational system... If you look at the Department of Education, it is the smallest Cabinet-level department in the federal government. It is less than 10 percent of the budget of the federal government. It was also just created one generation ago, in '79. It didn't exist before that. What that tells you is that education has not been a national priority in the US.
>
> Historically... a national educational policy may not have made sense [in such a large country], but in this day and age... the local educational system doesn't make sense anymore. We need a lot more national government in education; not less.... I don't think education today has anywhere close to the priority it should. And you know, if the budget is an indicator of priority, we see the military as being 10 times more important... The truth is that the military is important but what has made this country great is innovation and technology and its economic might. And this is mainly going to come from education... so we have to make education at the federal level a higher priority. No doubt about that.

According to Harvard professor Tony Wagner, however, this approach to reforming US education may not be sufficient. In his view, the challenges confronting US education today have become increasingly complex.

Wagner:

> Framing the problem, I think most people believe that the only real problem we have in education is raising the achievement of our disadvantaged students and getting more kids to college. My view is that if we merely aspire to that goal, we will leave *all* of our kids behind. I believe that need to fundamentally reenvision and rethink education for the twenty-first century, just as we had to rethink the one room school house for the industrial era.

From Wagner's perspective, the educational reform movement in the United States lacks a sufficient understanding of the problem that a knowledge-based economy poses. Rather than focusing on transmitting basic academic skills and competencies, he argues that educational reform needs to be more closely geared toward creativity and the *application* of knowledge.

Wagner:

> From my point of view, the fundamental reality is that we don't have an economy that can employ kids who graduate with the kinds of skills that our kids graduate with. Which is to say, skills that are kind of *low-level* intellectual and academic skills. We don't have an economy that can employ those people anymore. We don't have you know, blue-collar wage work. We don't have manufacturing. Post World War II, we were the largest manufacturing economy in the world. Today, it employs, what—not even ten million people.
>
> Right now, today, what most people don't realize—they say, "ah, the unemployment rate is going down, isn't that good news?" Well, you dig a little deeper and you realize it means *nothing*. Because, in point of fact, we have a smaller percentage of Americans working today in the labor force than at any time since 1978—when women first started entering the labor force in large numbers. 63 percent of Americans are either employed or looking for work. Then you subtract out the one's not looking for work, and you're barely over half of the country has a job. Then everybody says, "well, you send more kids to college and it's going to solve the problem." Well, you look at the combined under and unemployed rate of very recent college graduates, and it's disastrous. Depending on whose numbers you believe, the underemployment rate is well over 40 percent, with an additional 10 percent or more who are unemployed. By underemployment, I mean kids who have a job that doesn't require a BA, and doesn't pay BA degree wages. You know, we're worried about government debt in this country. The debt we really should be worried about is college graduate debt, which averages over 26 thousand dollars per kid—[debt that] can't be forgiven with bankruptcy.

## The Knowledge Economy: Implications for Educational Reform

Wagner's perspective is echoed by most of the experts interviewed for this book. The growing concern is that the US education system lacks the capacity to educate students for the kinds of competencies needed in the twenty-first century. As distinguished scholar and historian Cathy Davidson notes, there is a vast dissatisfaction with US education at all levels of the education system. In her view, schooling itself needs to be rethought today particularly with regard to the demands of a nascent revolution in digital technologies.

Davidson:

> I think we need a paradigm shift [in education]...I don't know teachers who like the current system. I don't know students who like the current system. I don't know administrators who like the current system. You know, I think people are really aware that the current system was developed out of a whole series of industrial age assumptions that are no longer pertinent and if we're creating—if the purpose of the institution is to support people's success in a certain kind of cultural environment—[then] that has changed. We need for institutions [to support] different institutional configurations.
>
> It's basically [that] what we know as school has existed for 120 years—and that's not very long. We're 15 years into the digital revolution... 15 years into the industrial revolution, we were just *inventing* the common schools. You know, Horace Mann in the 1840s inventing the common schools. So you know, it took a long time to invent the current system but, ah, the same kind of evolution will happen for the digital age. It has to, it's just not working.

While current educational policy reform focuses on testing academic achievement as the key output of schooling, the question many critics now ask is whether educational "reform" is sufficient.

Like Davidson, Wagner is critical of US education particularly with regard to what he describes as little more than incremental reform at the federal level. Linking US educational reform policies to what he characterizes as a faulty assessment about economic change, he offers a critique of the assumptions underlying education policy today.

Wagner:

> I think [President Obama's educational policies] have been a disaster. I think first and foremost driving states to evaluate teachers on the basis of standardized multiple choice test scores, for which students themselves have *no* accountability...as I said, I think it will drive the best teachers out of the profession. I think it is a *profoundly* unprofessional way of assessing teacher effectiveness.

In Wagner's view, the current national reforms based on data collection of student performance, including the implementation of common core standards, fall far short of the sort of innovation needed to transform US education. He elaborates:

> I think that it's not a matter of getting incrementally better at what we already do. It's a matter of fundamentally rethinking, reimagining—first and foremost—what are the outcomes that matter most? What should students know and be able to do, in an era where knowledge has become a commodity, and where the world doesn't care how much you know? *What the world cares about is what you can do with what you know.* And secondly, how do we motivate today's students to want to achieve levels of excellence? And then thirdly, how do we deal with the elephant in the room that nobody wants to talk about, the childhood poverty rate? This is the real story behind the achievement gap.

Wagner is right to point out that formal education has historically been geared to serve the needs of a highly stratified and predictable workforce. Beyond age-graded classes of fixed size and pacing, schooling is now tasked with being able to support competencies that drive postindustrial societies. Indeed, the results of the research supporting this book indicates that the current education system is in fact holding back transformation. The point here is that transforming schooling for KE is more complicated than simply reinforcing STEM disciplines through an enlarged testing regime. As Wagner observes, the key to transforming US education is reexamining the structure and provision of the education system itself.

Wagner:

> The world doesn't care how much you know, that's a commodity—you can look it up on the Internet. What the world cares about is what you can do with what you know. Which is a completely different and brand new education problem. We created our education systems in an era of knowledge scarcity. If you wanted to know something you had to go to the library. And if you wanted to know something that you had to sort of recall frequently you had to memorize it. Well, neither are true any longer. We now have a knowledge abundance system, not a knowledge scarcity system. That changes *everything*. It changes the purpose of education. You know, it used

to be that you had to go to a teacher because we teachers were the only ones in possession of those things called clay tablets, or then the papyrus reeds, or then those things called books—very expensive. And so you had to go through us to acquire the knowledge that we were in possession of. Well, now, knowledge is democratized; everybody has it. You don't need a teacher to get it. So then what's a teacher for? What's school for? These are brand new questions. And nobody is even asking them, let alone trying to answer them.

Wagner is not alone in his criticism of US education. For most of the experts interviewed for this book, the overarching view is that the kinds of reforms required for a knowledge economy are not being properly addressed in US education policy. As he observes, "you can't prepare kids for an innovation economy on an assembly line."

Wagner:

> Just looking at it from the point of view of jobs, just being very pragmatic about it. Structured routine jobs are all but gone out of our economy. The only ones that are left are local service jobs that pay minimum wage—service and retail. Manufacturing, white-collar, structured jobs are gone. *Even* jobs that have been considered comparatively *unstructured*—like law or accounting—are disappearing. And some kinds of medical practices are disappearing—like radiology. So what does that leave to employ people? Well, it leaves a large area of innovation and entrepreneurship. But that then demands that we prepare young people very very differently. You can't prepare kids for an innovation economy on an assembly line. And that's the core contradiction. We have factory model, assembly line, batch-processing schools that are holdovers from the industrial economy. But we don't have an industrial economy.

## Paradigm 2: Peer Production and the Network Economy

Despite the current influence of market-based thinking in educational reform policy, many of the experts interviewed for this book suggested that the increasing corporatization of schooling is a large part of the problem. Michel Bauwens, founder of the Peer-to-Peer Foundation, is perhaps the most pointed in his criticism.

Bauwens:

> I'm not sure all the following are connected to neoliberalism stricto sensu, but here are the main problems in education: (1) exaggerated standardization and testing in the primary grades, and hence a loss of focus on the whole individual, on critical thinking and on citizenship awareness; (2) commodification of education, which is increasingly seen as just obtaining skills for the market, and thus also, less and less attention to humanities and arts; (3) the problem of life-long debt dependency of students and how that constrains their choices of studies; (4) the increased control on teachers, heavier administrative burdens, and less freedom to teach how they see fit.

This is a view echoed by Wagner as well. Speaking to the issue of charter schools in the context of President Obama's educational policies, Wagner criticizes what he calls the "business theory of change":

> I think [it is a mistake] for the Obama administration to believe that charter schools are going to be a panacea for education. Essentially it's the business theory of change: the business theory of change is that the problem with education is the lack of competition so you create competition with charter schools and things will get better—number one. And number two—that what is really thwarting improvement of education is teacher unions, and so if you get rid of teacher unions that will be good too. And I see the Obama administration as kind of furthering both goals. Neither one of which is based on any evidence whatsoever...And I speak from experience. I actually helped start one of the first charter schools in Boston, and I believe that some of the best schools in this country happen to, in fact, be charter schools. But the research evidence says overwhelmingly [that] there are as many bad charter schools as there are good, and most of them are no better, no different.

Beyond neoliberal accounts of KE, there are, in fact, many alternative policy frameworks for shaping education. Alongside a transformation in mass industrial economy, there is a need for a corresponding transformation in the social and political philosophies that now guide education. Notwithstanding the fact that US educational policies fall short of many of the new social policies discussed in the context of Social Investment Theory (a point I will return to in chapter 6), there is a growing need to democratize access to education as a safeguard against widening social inequality. Critics of neoliberal readings of KE, for example, argue that the celebration of "knowledge workers" minimizes class stratification and ignores the systems of exploitation that underpin capitalist economy. More importantly, they miss the shifting architecture of socially mediated networks and a network society (Castells, 2000).

Critiquing the influence of neoliberalism on education, Bauwens argues that current educational reform policies only serve to expand social inequality.

Bauwens:

> I see two main different interlocking crises... The first issue has its roots in the educational model in industrial capitalism, that is, the centralized organization, the formatting of processes making education work like a factory, etc. The second issue derives from the pathological mode of neoliberal cognitive capitalism: the underfunding and destruction of equality-producing public education in favor of inequality-producing private education. This is, in other words, the destruction of any form of deep education that creates a full and rounded human being, and its replacement by purely functional "business" and "industrial" schooling.

For Bauwens, neoliberal capitalism is a pathological system that is predicated on false assumptions about human development. In fact, he takes issue with the very idea of KE:

> I actually reject the concept of the *knowledge economy*. Knowledge is not a scarce good, and should not artificially be made or kept scarce through legal repression or technological sabotage. So knowledge is by definition outside the economy of supply and demand, but is the general context through which humanity operates. Knowledge, culture, and science are part of the sphere of human abundance that the economy can profit from, and in turn can enable. The economy is the sphere of the circulation of scarce and rival goods, which exist to allow human culture and knowledge to thrive. So all humans should be educated for knowledge and culture as global citizens, and helped to create the economic value, which allows them to live and thrive and produce and exchange culture in their civic lives.

For theorists on KE as "cognitive capitalism," NE elides with notions of networked innovation and the generation and circulation of socially produced values and artifacts. As Hardt and Negri (2009) note, this does not mean "that the production of material goods, such as automobiles and steel [are] disappearing or even declining in quantity, but rather that their value is increasingly dependent on and subordinated to immaterial factors and goods" (p. 215). Here the object of production increasingly becomes subjectivity itself: "As biopolitical production becomes a dominant force of production, surplus value increasingly depends on the exploitation and expropriation of the creative and communicative circuits of culture—or what can be said to form the 'common'" (Means, 2011, p. 216).

For many, the NE paradigm represents a new frontier in socially mediated work and learning. Pointing to the importance of shared collaboration in the development of use value over exchange value, Bauwens outlines an alternative account of postindustrial society. Indeed, he rejects the idea of "human capital" and related notions of exchange value (exchanging labor for capital). In his view, human capital does not subsist in the individual alone. Rather, it is the excrescence or outgrowth of socially mediated networks.

Bauwens:

> We need to put use value at the core of our society and economy again, and consider exchange value as a mere means to an end. As we move away from the commodification and instrumentalization of the human, we can start seeing ourselves integratively, as a set of "capitals" that can be developed over time through self-work, and coproduction, including relational capital, knowledge capital, social capital, and so forth.

The key point is that common value creation transcends the market as a plane of social activity (Hardt and Negri, 2009). In this paradigm, learning is increasingly viewed as interdependent with mass participation (Davidson and Goldberg, 2010). Building on discourses that view ICTs as bridging a global society, knowledge and learning are linked to discussions on community. In Cormier's (2010) terms, the *community is the curriculum*. Less driven by knowledge transmission and more closely joined to communities-of-practice, learning is understood in terms of "rhizomatic" networks. For this reason, education is seen as deeply interconnected with peer production and the co-creation of value. From this perspective, peer production is

understood as the primary source of value and a fundamentally new logic and/or a new stage in history:
Bauwens:

> Our basic hypothesis is that peer-to-peer networks engender a new type of sociality that is fundamentally transforming our societies. In particular, we focus on the self-aggregation of people around the common creation of value, based on shareable IP, which we call peer production, and its associated modes of governance and property. We monitor both the bottom-up institutionalizations of such processes, and also the adaptation of the existing institutions to such challenges. We consider three paradigms to be key: openness, focusing on open and free contributions; participatory processes or "deep democracy"; and the commons or sharing paradigms, which concerns the results.

Indeed, Bauwens is unambiguous about the democratic potential of peer production:

> In the context of the emerging system of peer production, citizens should be enabled to participate in a contributory economy that rests on contributed knowledge. This means: (1) discovering your passion; (2) learning skills to cocreate; 3) finding ways to contribute to the general welfare. So the key is to find the intersection between passion, skills, and what is needed by concrete human communities.

Speaking to the need to rethink education for NE, he suggests that the challenge today is to transmit the new tools and practices that make accessing networks equally available to all.
Bauwens:

> The immediate effect of networked learning is that it favors those who have learned autonomy, but still leaves broad layers of the student and non-student population behind. Thus, while it enables many, it also in the short term creates new inequalities between those that have the means and skills to use networks, and those that have difficulties with this. Thus part of educational reform must also be the sharing of means and skills to create equality of access, and the cognitive and social skills needed for this type of participation.

However, not all experts interviewed were predisposed to positive characterizations of the NE paradigm. In Donald Brinkman's view, for example, it is a mistake to interpret contemporary innovations in technology as somehow detached from the institutional realities and contexts in which they are embedded. Brinkman, a program manager at Microsoft Research, is critical of the exaggerated expectations of networked collaboration. He points out that peer production remains highly dependent on hierarchical organization, citing the democratic decline of touchstone projects like Wikipedia.

This is true, of course. While network-mediated learning leverages agency and autonomy in the context of "situated" networks of artifacts, technologies, and people (Brown et al, 1989; Lave, 1998; Lave & Wenger, 1991; Varela, 1991), this largely depends on socially mediated access to these networks (Vygotsky, 1978). As Selwyn (2009, p. 92) reminds us, learning is now strongly connected to an individual's capacity to access embedded information sources.

## The Network Economy: Implications for Educational Reform

In the NE paradigm, education is perhaps best framed as community participation. Indeed, OS projects such as Wikipedia and Linux, and social platforms such as Facebook and Twitter, are viewed as illustrations of the rising importance of networked connectivity across institutions and practices (Granovetter, 1973). Beyond a market model based on designing schooling for an industrial society, NE suggests that the needs of a socially mediated knowledge economy may well force schools to become reconfigured around open networks and socially mediated learning practices.

Bauwens:

> The traditional education of industrial society was about creating packaged goods. Clearly defined skills and knowledge so that the products of education would fit in the economy. But a knowledge society needs much more creative, transdisciplinary individuals

who can creatively co-construct and problem solve in productive communities that are much more fluid than before. More importantly, modern generations crave above all to have meaningful occupations. And since the current system insufficiently responds to this, many are creating their own occupations, through new forms of ethical and social entrepreneurship that create value but also social good. Their learning process to achieve this value is now mostly by stealth, through the interstices of the educational system and through the access to networked communities, where a lot of self and peer learning takes place. This kind of parallel education needs to become a much bigger part of the new educational mainstream. I would suggest that in the new educational systems, co-creation in productive communities is part of the educational practice.

Where the traditional method of expert instruction requires significant time and resources, collaborative problem-solving in the form of wikis, blogs, and online communities are restructuring the way people build and use knowledge (Brown et al., 1989; Brown and Adler, 2008). But, as Bauwens explains, the bureaucratic structure of factory schooling remains inhospitable to experimentation with this social dynamic.

What is obvious is that learning and education are becoming more closely linked to what Cormier (2010) describes as a "rhizomatic model" of learning. From this perspective, curriculum design should be less driven by the predefined inputs of experts and more driven by students engaged in the learning process itself. This includes "a more discursive rhizomatic approach to knowledge discovery," based on both the exploration of an established knowledge canon and the negotiation of what in fact qualifies as knowledge (Cormier, 2010, p. 515).

As Cormier suggests, the community acts as the curriculum, spontaneously shaping both itself and the subject of its learning in the same way that the rhizome responds to changing environmental conditions. He (2010) observes,

> community as curriculum is not meant as a simple alternative to the package version of learning. It is, rather, meant to point to the learning that takes place on top of that model and to point to the strategies for continuing learning throughout a career. There is a

> base amount of knowledge that is required to be able to enter a community, and there are methods for acquiring the specific kinds of literacy needed to learn within a specific community. A learner acquires basic forms of literacy and associates with different peer groups. Networks begin to form and, occasionally, communities develop. Knowledge is created and sometimes discarded as the community interacts. Knowledge does not develop and spread from and through concentric circles. There are no "plastics" to be learned and no canon to consult to ensure that a new skill has been acquired. Knowledge is a rhizome, a snapshot of interconnected ties in constant flux that is evaluated by its success in context. (pp. 516–517)

Perhaps a clear sign of the increasing influence of the NE paradigm is that it is becoming part of the literature on educational reform itself (Iiyoshi & Kumar, 2010; OECD, 2007c). Networked collaboration, it is now argued, is highly conducive to learning and innovation because production is now grounded in self-organizing systems of collective intelligence (Lévy, 1997; Ito et al., 2008).

## Paradigm 3: Creative Practice and the Creative Economy

One obvious question that emerges from discussions on KE is whether it represents a fundamental break with capitalist economy. According to Richard Florida, director of the Martin Prosperity Institute at the University of Toronto, KE is in fact something closer to a new stage of capitalist economy than a discrete break with capitalism, per se.

Florida:

> I see the knowledge economy as an evolution from [the industrial economy]. So in my earliest work I was very much concerned with the debate over Fordism and what comes after Fordism—so called post-Fordism (especially the regulation school or regulación in France and Europe). The argument went…Fordism, mass

production, industrial Fordism, has reached its limits and a new system was emerging to replace it. Many of those people were looking at the flexible industrial districts [in] Italy or perhaps the Silicon Valley, as exemplars of this. People like Allen Scott and AnnaLee Saxenian, people who I very, very much admire and have learned a lot from.

In my work... [I] did detailed examinations of Silicon Valley and Route 128, we actually embarked on a project studying Japanese economic production and organization and then the Japanese transplant companies in the United States. And we concluded that, in fact, what looked like it was going to evolve away from Fordism and to post-Fordism was what Japanese companies were doing on the factory floor... [In fact], the inspiration for [theories] of the creative economy do not come necessarily from Apple or from Google, or for high-tech Silicon Valley companies (although I think they do some things very well). [And it] certainly doesn't come from trying to understand arts and culture or even diversity, as one of my critics put it... I don't think that at all. In fact, I argued that [the Japanese] method of economic organization and social organization that Toyota perfected... harnessing the talent, innovation, creativity, and productivity of [the] shop floor workers [was the key to success].

For advocates of CE, human creativity is viewed as the key to unlocking postindustrial societies. Florida describes this as a shift from quantity to quality, and from top-down to bottom-up organizations.

Florida:

So in this sense, the "creative economy," as I see it, is a... *break* with the industrial era [and] classic canonical Fordist industrial organization [in which] workers were seen as cogs in the machine—as backs, as brains, as brawn. But I think the spirit and inspiration for the creative economy actually comes from advances made in manufacturing. And... I actually think what Toyota does with manufacturing is very in tune with the evolution of a creative economy and [with] what Apple and Google and IDEO do in design... So in a sense, it's quantity leading up to quality and ultimately something new, but really it's born from the belly of the old industrial order.

Moving past the managerial steering systems built for the industrial economy, creativity, and creative practice are viewed as critical to CE (Howkins, 2001; Zhao, 2012b). This includes a particular emphasis on entrepreneurship and intersubjectivity in the "gale of creative destruction" that enables new social and cultural forms. Building on Schumpeter (2008 [1942]), CE emphasizes the blending and combination of currently existing technologies in the continual replacement of old industries with new industries. Citing Marx, Florida points to the growing link between affect and labor:

> You know if I go back and read my Marx, I see that Marx was very concerned with the physical production and the physical labor of people and how that was alienated. I think that he saw physical production and alienation as part of this intersubjectivity that makes people similar. I actually think human creativity is what makes us more *alike*. I look at *Grundrisse* and say, "Oh, my God!" Marx already almost thought of that. So I think there's this very basic thing in creativity that is democratizing...I actually think the logic of economic history is on our side...I actually think that the logic of economic growth is pushing us towards a mode of production that requires further and more expansive human participation.

For Florida, the roots of this evolving cultural milieu lie outside the market or formal institutions altogether. Accordingly, new emergent forms of creativity are interdependent with larger cultural systems that are associated with meta-changes in postindustrial society.

Florida:

> What people don't understand is the rise of the movement for cultural openness is [systemic]. I look at the 60s as a giant temper tantrum associated with the fact that the energy of creative and innovative people couldn't be harnessed by the old industrial order. So we had James Dean and Elvis Presley and Jimi Hendrix and it was like a giant temper tantrum...The real legacy of the 60s isn't Woodstock; it's the rise of the new system of production organization and innovation in Silicon Valley which found ways to harness that kind of thing, and I think even more so the new order really is born in the belly of industrial society. And I would argue that the

most important company to understand the creative economy was Toyota. But now it's something new and different.

For advocates of CE, creativity is seen as the key to the continual invention of new products, new markets, and new forms of labor productivity. Indeed, this implies something more than simply human capital formation. In Florida's view, the scale of this change points to the need to rethink institutions that support human capital development—especially systems of education. Beyond HCT, he describes CE as a level above human capital.
Florida:

> This is somewhat different I think than, human capital. Specifically, I mean, human capital seems to be skills that are already known... But a lot of what the creative class brings to the table is something that we don't necessarily know ahead of time. So they're creating new job skills along with the work they do in it. As much as they need formal education in there—human capital is clearly required, [this is] something beyond. It's a level up from human capital.

Like Florida, scholars and theorists such as Daniel Pink (2005), Ken Robinson (2001), and John Maeda (2006) emphasize the need for enhancing creativity in education, particularly in relation to associated notions of talent formation and self-expression. Florida, for example, suggests that the future of education in a knowledge-based economy may well move outside formal schooling altogether:

> You know, it may be that creativity is just too different than education. Perhaps we need some new kind of institution that is very different than what we have now. I think that's a first order problem and I just know that what we have now isn't working. People are not necessarily learning in school, they're learning despite school. I think no one is willing to really throw that out there and if I have to track my own intellectual development I would say (now it's hard to reconstruct your life), but I would say I learned despite school not because of school. I can think of very few things I learned in school... I think we need to really, really think long and hard about what that set of institutions would look like for young creative people.

## The Creative Economy: Implications for Educational Reform

If it is true that CE demands fresh thinking about workforce capacities and institutions, then it should follow that the growing rhetoric on the economic need for creativity would move policymakers to push for experimentation and a more expansive view of schooling. Sadly, this has not been the case. Indeed, if what we want is a system that helps students to become self-directed and intrinsically capable of acquiring new knowledge and skills, then we must first recognize key problems within the education system itself. As Florida suggests, schools must become places where human creativity is cultivated and can flourish because modern societies "can no longer succeed—or even tread water—with an education system handed down to us from the industrial age" (Florida, 2005, p. 254).

The implications for creative practices and creative work in transforming education are significant to education policy for a variety of reasons. Indeed, there are very real questions about whether the education system as a whole is doing more harm than good. As Means (2011) notes,

> it would seem logical that calls for creativity and innovation would present a substantive challenge to a narrow industrial model of schooling based on stratified, centralized and institutionally rationalized forms of school organization and curriculum. One would imagine that schooling for the creative economy would want to draw on, harness, and develop human capabilities while promoting greater autonomy and equity. The reality has been somewhat different. (p. 219)

In truth, the general lack of "entrepreneurial" thinking around K-12 education itself stands in stark contrast to much of the contemporary rhetoric on educational reform (Zhao, 2012b). Beyond discussions on skills development, for example, CE refocuses attention on issues of subjectivity, self-actualization, and talent formation in the context of creative practice.

What discussions on CE point out is that building educational reform around notions of human capital formation undermines the needed flexibility for developing students who are actually capable of autonomous creativity and entrepreneurship. This overlaps constructivist notions of education, rooted in the work of John Dewey (1975), Maria Montessori (1964), Jean Piaget (1954), Lawrence Kohlberg (1969), as well as the philosophical thinking of Jean-Jacques Rousseau[1] and Romantic notions of progressive education. All of which suggests that educational reform might be better served by focusing on critical thinking, collaboration, and problem-solving as a foundation to CE.

## Paradigm 4: Green Innovation and the Green Economy

In addition to the Creative Economy and the Network Economy, there is widespread political and economic interest in "clean technologies" and a Green Economy. Indeed, the notion of clean technologies is now driving an international competition around clean energy generation with many governments attempting to capitalize on green innovation.

Notwithstanding the fact that the definition of GE remains in flux, much of the discussion on green economic growth is directly linked to the elimination of fossil fuels and the long-term production of low-carbon, renewable energy (wind, solar, geothermal, and biomass). Directly overlapping discussions on climate change, GE is viewed as a foundation for a postindustrial civilization. For Tony Seba and many other Silicon Valley entrepreneurs, GE is seen as a major historical disruption in energy production and consumption with significant market potential.

Seba:

> I've been developing or helping to develop solar power plants and wind power plants and I also teach on these subjects...I think that over the next 10 or 15 years we will go through the most massive disruption in our society since the first industrial revolution. I think the changes that are coming are just massive [because] there are a

handful of technologies right now that are improving exponentially and will disrupt both transportation and energy as we know it...

In fact, the recent rush of stimulus spending around the world includes significant investments in GE. These investments are seen by many as critical to the future prosperity of advanced economies. In the United States, the Obama administration's stimulus bill dedicated $71 billion to clean energy funding, with an additional $20 billion for loan guarantees and tax incentives to support clean energy projects. This included investments in a *Unified National Smart Grid* linking all of the nation's local electrical networks that have been upgraded to smart grids. Seba, however, is critical of the US energy policies.

Seba:

> I'm fairly disappointed [with President Obama's energy policies]. I don't think he has an energy policy actually. He goes on the record proudly saying we are generating more oil than we ever have, and we are generating more natural gas than we ever have, and you know he tripled the budget for nuclear energy, and so on and so forth. So I would say that he hasn't emphasized clean energy *at all*.
>
> The main policy mechanism that has pushed at least solar energy on the national level is the investment tax credit and that was actually a Bush [era] policy...And so I don't see Obama as a clean energy guy at all. He hasn't pushed back on clean energy like the Bush administration or the Reagan administration. But he hasn't moved us forward either. You know, half of all the solar in the United States is in California. That is because of state policies. That is because both Governor Brown and Governor Schwarzenegger pushed for the Renewable Portfolio Standards and that's because we voted for climate change law at a state level...That gives you an indication of where the leadership for clean energy is coming from. It's clearly not coming from Washington.

As Seba points out, reducing global warming and enhancing resource management are strong reasons to take the idea of GE seriously. In fact, evidence from climate science points to the need for coordinated energy policy, including a broad portfolio of active technologies and regulatory management. The limitations of past

US policy, however, suggest that the United States has a long way to go.
Seba:

> Germany has pushed solar and wind legislation since 2000. Germany by itself has been a third of all the installed solar in the world. And you know, because of the learning curve that has meant that the cost of solar has gone down *really* substantially since then. Also because China has invested massively in solar. Basically costs have gone down dramatically just over the last three years. The costs have gone down by more than 80 percent. But its been driven mostly by Germany and China, not by the US. Having said that, solar is now at the point that it is cheaper than grid energy in hundreds of markets around the world without subsidies. So, yeah, we are on the cusp of a major disruption of energy worldwide.

In Seba's view, technology may be essential to green innovation but strategic public policy is critical. Growing concern about climate change and the impact of carbon dioxide emissions has made GE a predominant feature of discussions on educational reform. Seba argues that this discussion needs to also consider substantial changes in the structure and practice of education itself. Echoing the arguments of other experts, he suggests that education systems need to be redesigned to enable postindustrial competencies:
Seba:

> Most of our early education is still delivered in an agricultural or industrial way. Today we need to educate creative thinkers and we need to do that from the time they are kids. It's not about rote learning, its not about learning *stuff*, its about creative thinking. And especially in the "knowledge economy," an educated person starts from the time a person is 1-2-3 years old. Not from the time they get into college. An educated person needs to know how to consume and generate knowledge... [including] how to generate and consume knowledge about knowledge... [And] with machine learning, AI, robotics, and so on, we also need to teach kids to use the tools to generate and consume knowledge.

While environmental policy in the United States has mainly focused on educating (and sometimes miseducating) the private sector about its environmental impact, what the United States has lacked most is a robust public policy for coordinating a coherent strategy for GE. This includes a robust education policy for GE as well.

## The Green Economy: Implications for Educational Reform

Unlike other paradigms of KE, GE is unique in that it speaks to the need for a fundamental transformation in industrial economy. In truth, 85 percent of energy in the United States comes from fossil fuels (petroleum, coal, and natural gas). Indeed, while the United States produces 10 percent of the world's oil, it consumes one quarter of the world's total supply. Moreover, until recently 70 percent of that oil was imported from abroad. What is ironic is that America's high-tech society is built on top of a fossil fuel economy of oil, coal, and natural gas.

The challenges associated with GE suggest that a redesign of education that responds to the scale of the problem of climate change is now critical to reforming US education. Building on this thinking, Rifkin (2011) makes a compelling case for education playing a critical role in empowering new generations of students and citizens for GE. He outlines several critiques of contemporary mass education and makes specific suggestions on changes to the methodological and pedagogical assumptions underlying contemporary schooling.

This includes developing curriculum supporting "advanced information, nano- and biotechnologies, Earth sciences, ecology, and systems theory as well as vocational skills, including manufacturing and marketing renewable energy technologies, transforming buildings into mini power plants, installing hydrogen and other storage technologies, laying out intelligent utility networks...and the like" (p. 231).

Just as schooling should be redesigned around ICTs, Rifkin (2011) argues that schools should be physically and conceptually redesigned around renewable energy generation and environmental stewardship. In addition to professional and vocational skills, this means moving beyond a utilitarian view of nature. As Rifkin observes, the "notion that the primary mission of education is to turn out productive workers is grounded on a particular notion of human nature that was spawned in the Enlightenment at the very beginning of the industrial era" (p. 233).

Building on Cormier's notion of the community as curriculum, Rifkin adds the necessity for including the "biosphere as learning environment" in preparing students to "think and act as part of a shared biosphere" (p. 248). He writes:

> Our ideas about education invariably flow from our perception of reality and our conception of nature—especially our assumptions about human nature and the meaning of the human journey... Our emerging sense of biosphere consciousness coincides with discoveries in evolutionary biology, neurocognitive science, and child development that reveal that people are biologically predisposed to be empathic—that our core nature is not rational, detached, acquisitive, aggressive, and narcissistic, as many Enlightenment philosophers suggested, but rather, affectionate, highly social, cooperative, and interdependent... New teaching models designed to transform education from a competitive contest to a collaborative and empathic learning experience are emerging as schools and colleges try and reach a generation that has grown up on the Internet and is used to interacting in open social networks where information is shared rather than hoarded. (Rifkin, 2011, pp. 234–236)

Interestingly, Rifkin's suggestions for transforming education echo those of Bauwens (2009) and Cormier (2010) in describing highly networked educational environments designed more closely to mirror complex social dynamics.

## Conclusion: Rethinking Education Policy

While it is certainly true that education has always been a complicated struggle to manage competing sets of goals linked to a wide assortment of philosophical positions on human development (Gardner, 1983; Miller 1997; Crain 2000), it would seem that the challenges associated with KE are of a fundamentally different order. What is obvious from these interviews is that there is a wide range of competencies needed for invigorating postindustrial societies in the twenty-first century. This includes new education systems that support networked collaboration (Araya and Peters, 2010), reinvigorated artistic practices (Robinson, 2001), and a comprehensive focus on environmental stewardship (Rifkin, 2011).

Perhaps the main problem facing educational reform today, however, is that there is no single vision or definition of KE through which to redesign education. Indeed, a growing surplus of underemployed knowledge workers calls into question public policies that promote LLL in the context of a global knowledge economy (Longworth and Davies, 1996; OECD, 2007a). Beyond human capital theory, there is now the looming challenge of labor automation and yet there remains a paucity of literature that examines this ongoing social transformation.

As Keynes (1930) famously wrote, "We are being afflicted with a new disease...namely, *technological unemployment.* This means unemployment due to our discovery of means of economising the use of labour outrunning the pace at which we can find new uses for labour." Historically, new jobs have followed in the wake of technological change. Just as factory labor displaced farm labor, so labor in the service sector expanded in the face of globalization. Today, however, growing technological unemployment linked to artificial intelligence and industrial robotics is undermining conventional theories on labor churn. Moreover, technological innovation in the form of industrial robotics, artificial intelligence, and genetic engineering is making all labor—including educated labor—less valuable. Even if new jobs and new products and services emerge over the long term, acute social dislocation will grow alongside significant income stratification in the short term.

Put simply, the question today is whether technology will in fact facilitate newer and more innovative forms of labor or simply continue to subsume labor entirely. In the context of education, this has made older industrialized notions of formal education increasingly superfluous. What we do know is that rather than framing educational reform in terms of the needs of an industrial society, educational policies must now drive toward the new and varied needs of a computational society. Beyond basic numeracy and literacy, we now need to support competencies that include network-mediated collaboration and entrepreneurial innovation.

In the final chapter of this book, I make conclusions regarding the strengths and weaknesses of contemporary US educational reform and offer suggestions for improving educational policy through social investment. Taken as a whole, it is my view that the key problem with educational reform today is that policy-driven narratives on KE assume a theoretical homogeneity, when in reality KE is highly multifaceted and variegated. Additionally, while it may be true that human capital development is necessary to ensure economic competitiveness, it is also true that human capital theory is not sufficient for supporting educational reform over the long term. Alongside human capital formation, there are emergent challenges related to creativity and innovation that supersede the value of skills-driven reforms alone.

# Chapter 6

# Rethinking US Education Policy

Building on a critical analysis of contemporary education policy, I argue in this book that accelerating trends in economic theory now shape a particular discourse on educational reform. More specifically, I suggest that educational reform policies are based upon contradictory readings of the knowledge economy. More than mere philosophies of economy, these "paradigms" of KE represent overlapping ontologies that seek to define and explain an extensive transformation of modern industrial society. Unpacking four of these paradigms, I have argued that there is a need to reexamine the basic assumptions that now guide US education policy. More precisely, I have argued that there are substantial differences between conceptualizations of KE that in turn produce contradictory policy narratives.

My purpose in defining these economic discourses as paradigms is to develop a deeper understanding of the features and logics of KE and to encourage the development of a new policy framework for US education. Mapping the contours of the Neoliberal Knowledge Economy, the Creative Economy, the Network Economy, and the Green Economy—and looking specifically at the import of these paradigms for shaping US education—I have argued for the need to move past neoliberal social policies. Beyond simple criticism of neoliberalism, my goal has been to reexamine education policy in light of emergent challenges facing postindustrial societies.

## Toward a New Framework for Education

Informed by research data that includes public policy texts on US education produced by the Obama administration and interviews with scholars and experts on the study of KE, the purpose of this book has been to explore sociopolitical proposals for rethinking US educational reform. Despite the rising value of higher education, the United States now finds itself struggling to improve the quality of its human capital. Whereas the United States was the leader in high school and college graduation rates over much of the twentieth century, its relative standing has since peaked and declined (Goldin and Katz, 2008).

According to most analysts, the root of the problem is the failure of the US school system to ensure high-quality education for poor and marginalized students. However, it is my view that this is only part of the problem. Notwithstanding the fact that returns on investments in education over the last century have been substantial to US economic growth, the truth is that the US education system today has become ossified. In fact, as Acemoglu and Autor (2012) observe, a pervasive decline in the quality of US human capital cannot be reasonably explained by a decline within the US educational system alone. Indeed, this decline is part and parcel of a widespread investment in neoliberal social policies and a drift toward plutocratic policymaking.

Even a cursory analysis of contemporary educational reform reveals a deep concern with transforming US society and economy in the face of systemic economic change. The growing consensus today is that rising demands placed on US education are not simply rooted in a temporary economic downturn, but in a permanent sea change in the structure of the global economy. As advanced economies enter into what may eventually be described as the "Automation Age," many now doubt the long-term efficacy of US education policy. In the face of the Great Recession, for example, it has become painfully obvious that the current education system is not equipped to mitigate dislocation in the labor market. Even as millions of jobs have been generated since the 2008 crisis, the majority of these jobs have been very low wage. Building on these concerns, this final chapter offers near- and long-term recommendations for transforming US education policy with the ultimate goal of reconsidering the economic philosophy that now drives US educational reform.

## Education Policy for a Postindustrial Economy

In truth, any analysis of educational reform requires a theory of political economy. Indeed, one of the main issues in educational reform today is the application of ICTs in the continuous restructuring of knowledge-based work and learning (Dyer-Witheford, 2000; Autor, Levy, & Murnane, 2003). As ICTs continue to standardize and codify labor, knowledge workers are increasingly forced to acquire more knowledge to stay ahead. Notwithstanding the fact that new tools engender changes in the way people interact, communicate, and collaborate (Siemens, 2004), the growing standardization of knowledge work elides with a long-term process of labor automation. This "digital Taylorism" (Brown, Lauder, and Ashton, 2010) is critical to understanding the future of education policy.

Just as twentieth-century education systems formed the socioeconomic foundations for an expanding industrial society, so today twenty-first-century education systems are viewed as foundations for an expanding postindustrial society (Goldin and Katz, 2008; Lauder et al., 2008). At the same time, mounting demand to augment human capital has triggered a wide-ranging debate about the kinds of skills and competencies needed to drive postindustrial societies. What is clear is that technological change linked to theories on endogenous growth suggest that technological innovation is increasingly favoring a "computer literate" labor force.

It is no exaggeration to suggest that increasing technological change is emerging as a daunting challenge with few obvious long-term solutions (Brynjolfsson and McAfee, 2014). As middle-class jobs continue to be eliminated by technology, the obvious question is "what can education do to mitigate this process?" Although it was once true that US public schools were effective vehicles for distributing the sociotechnical skills needed for an Age of Industry (numeracy, literacy, symbol manipulation), it is now the case that these institutions are simply not equipped to provide the skills needed for an Age of Innovation (Scardamalia, 2002; Bereiter, 2002b; Araya & Peters, 2010).

In response to SBTC, the Obama administration has made significant effort to redesign US education policy in line with a more pronounced national innovation framework. This includes a strategic focus on domestic investments in education aimed at boosting long-term economic performance. Much as the previous administration, President Obama has concentrated on enlarging the role of the federal government in order to raise the quality of public education. Unfortunately, this political gambit has resulted in educational reform measures that lack the strategic foresight necessary to resolve rising underemployment. Indeed, many critical scholars argue that current education policies are too narrowly focused on accountability and testing at the expense of creativity and innovation:

> Invocations to unleash creativity and innovation in educational contexts appear to stand in tension with the realities of the reorganization of education along the lines of privatization, audits and testing, standardization, and the marginalization of the social sciences and the humanities—processes that place limits on knowledge production and the free and cooperative exchange of ideas. (Means, 2011, pp. 224–225)

Where formal education continues to focus on inculcating basic "reading, writing, and mathematics" skills, advanced computational technologies now demand workers who are skilled in critical analysis and the creative application of new knowledge. Where international benchmarks such as PISA and TIMSS were once honest reflections of the quality of education within a country or region, today these tests simply offer less value. Consider, for example, this aggregate forecast of STEM professions by the US Bureau of Labor Statistics (2013). What is obvious is that the use and application of computing and ICTs is becoming the basis for leading professions in the twenty-first century (figure 6.1).

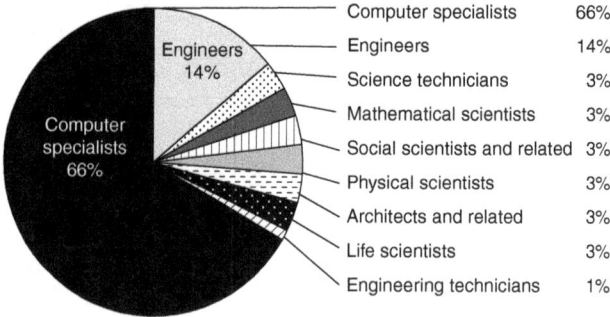

**Figure 6.1**  New STEM professions through 2020.
*Source*: Data from US Bureau of Labor Statistics (2013).

## Educational Reform for the Near Term: Augmenting Human Intelligence

Part of the answer to reforming US education over the near term involves leveraging digital technologies to augment human intelligence. Even as computers automate routine labor, they also amplify opportunities for work that requires creativity, problem-solving, and social collaboration (Autor, 2014). Put differently, while computers excel at many logical functions, they are simply not as efficient or effective as human beings at tasks requiring flexibility, creativity, and judgment. Developing an education system that bridges human and computer intelligence, for example, offers a potential near-term resolution to the challenges of labor automation. Much as Douglas Engelbart (1962) first described, computational technologies represent an opportunity to expand human intelligence in new and unexplored ways. This includes developing more interactive and personalized learning environments conducive to advancing creativity and experimentation.

Collins & Weiner (2010), for example, propose a new interdisciplinary category blending education and information science in the form of education informatics. Although the origins of informatics[1] can be traced to the mid-twentieth century, the term "educational informatics" is quite recent (Stewart, 2000). Collins & Weiner define education informatics as "the application of technology to discovering and communicating education information" (p. 1). In their view, the idea of education informatics is much broader in scope than educational technology:

> Information technology is key to knowledge diffusion, but understanding and developing human interaction, human behavior, and information use and exchange are also essential (Pinelli & Barclay, 1998, p. 168). Just as educational psychologists and learning theorists studied the potential for television and other technologies leading to the development and delivery of educational programs and services, so too must they examine the application of information technology at all levels, from scholarly communication models developing within higher education, to the social networking systems and information seeking practices of school children, in order to inform the creation and use of education information systems. (p. 1)

Educating for an era of smart technologies suggests the need for new thinking on ICT proficiency and the experimental use of advanced computational technologies across schools and universities. Much as the National Educational Technology Plan (US Department of Education, 2010c) points out, this will certainly include the use of gaming and simulations in concert with network-mediated environments. The value of gaming to education, for example, is that it provides a means for self-diagnostics and enhanced user control in the context of immersive environments.

Part of the challenge ahead is simply to move beyond a preoccupation with measuring basic skills and content in favor of schools that directly leverage ICTs in support of creative innovation. Much as the one-room schoolhouse of the nineteenth century gave way to a national education system in the twentieth century, so today the factory school must give way to new systems of digitally mediated learning. Beyond industrial hierarchies based upon social reproduction, educational systems must be redesigned to drive sustained personalized learning.

The truth is that educational systems today are undergoing a highly disruptive transformation anchored to a revolution in computational technologies. In contrast to learning factories, what we now require are learning networks that allow students to directly engage with one another in the building and transforming of ideas and social practices. Indeed, the central problem with US educational reform today is a misplaced focus on mobilizing systems of measurement and discipline in an era that demands risk and experimentation. Beyond neoliberal social policies and shortsighted investments in human capital formation, US education policy must now begin to reconsider its basic foundations.

An interdisciplinary field like education informatics, for example, points the way to user-driven information systems that can support digitally mediated learning, instruction, and knowledge discovery. Building on cloud computing and high-bandwidth systems, these learning environments could provide ubiquitous access to knowledge while at the same time bridging formal and informal learning (Stricker et al., 2009). The hard reality is that the Internet has begun forcing postindustrial societies into a complex "phase transition." As Waks (2013) observes, this is a shift from linear systems to complex dynamic systems and it points to a dramatic restructuring of systems of cultural production (Siemens, 2004; Barabási, 2002). The consequences of this phase transition are difficult to predict, but we do know that the batch-processing system that underlies schooling is now antiquated. What is obvious, for example, is that education systems must be predicated upon creativity and collaboration rather than cultural consumption.

Indeed, responding to the needs of a network society by retrofitting factory schools with computational technologies is not a solution to the needs of a knowledge-based society. Rather, we must begin to reimagine education in light of the affordances of ICT networks. This begins with reconsidering the transmission model that is so deeply embedded in the fabric of industrial schools. If competency in the use of artifacts within existing cultural systems is the goal of industrial education, then cultural production and the reshaping of cultural systems will be the goal of education going forward (Araya and Peters, 2010).

## Educational Reform for the Long-Term: Education as Social Transformation

Moving beyond the logics of mass production and a world of iterative cultural change, education must be redesigned to fit the needs of a computational knowledge economy (Wolfram, 2010). In addition to adapting education to technology, the real challenge today is to reframe the institutional and pedagogical structures that constitute schooling. The underlying problem is that factory schools have evolved from older institutions designed for different eras. These include the monastery as a knowledge repository and the factory as a command production system (Leadbeater, 2000).

Much as the Industrial Revolution transformed physical labor, the Computational Revolution is now transforming cognitive labor (Beniger, 1986). Perhaps it is not surprising that this is the very same challenge facing corporate institutions as well. As corporations seek to use ICTs to harness the subjectivity of workers, they risk undermining the very autonomous capacities that produce innovation in the first place (Hardt and Negri, 2009). As McNeely and Wolverton (2008) explain, this reflects a dramatic shift in the very meaning of "literacy." Indeed, this epistemological shift in the structure of knowledge reflects "far-reaching changes in economics, culture, and technology [which now] raise questions about the production, preservation and transmission of knowledge" (p. xii).

Many thinkers argue that massive open online courses (MOOCs) will enable a kind of global revolution in education at near-zero cost (Rifkin, 2014). In reality, it is more likely that the distributed networks that enable digital technologies are the key to redesigning schooling. Put simply, it is not merely formal education that must be rethought, but the ideologies supporting mass industrial civilization as a whole. The reality is that technology is not simply transforming how we produce and manage knowledge and learning, it is transforming how we produce value altogether. Indeed, the rise of computational technologies is fomenting a radical shift in the way our society is now organized and governed.

The central challenge we face today is that knowledge-based societies are highly computational. Together software algorithms, computer-aided design, data analytics, and machine learning have begun to revolutionize the institutions and social practices that anchor postindustrial societies. Some thinkers suggest that the scale of this technological transformation may even eventually outstrip human cognitive capacities altogether (Kurzweil, 2006). If we accept forecasts suggesting rapid labor mechanization over the next two decades, then we can safely assume that postindustrial economies are entering a new era in which labor markets and education may no longer be tightly coupled (Frey and Osborne, 2013).

The overarching policy response to this social transformation from the Obama administration has been to focus on leveraging education to manage against labor redundancy. But rising unemployment *across* a range of industries is making this strategy less tenable. Where human capital theory may offer value to educational reform in the short term, it offers less value for rethinking education systems over the long term. The truth is that transferring a fixed body of knowledge and practices from experts to amateurs is becoming contradictory to a society increasingly driven by entrepreneurial innovation. Moving beyond the hierarchical systems of the Industrial Age, students must now leverage networked collaboration to solve real world problems. Indeed, any new mode of education will involve more than merely broadcasting a discrete set of vocational skills; it will involve scaffolding real-world problem-solving as part of the larger continuum of "public knowledge building" (Scardamalia, 2002).

Where the Industrial Age introduced a level of machine-based innovation that revolutionized physical labor, the computer age is now threatening to displace large swathes of the labor force altogether. Notwithstanding the fact that conventional economic models assume that new jobs will emerge and replace the jobs displaced by technology, there is growing concern that accelerating computing power makes this argument less tenable. What is clear is that productivity growth has risen substantially over the past two decades, even as social institutions have begun to ossify. Despite the vast wealth created in recent decades, the lion's share of this wealth has been consumed by a very small elite.

What seems obvious is that strategies for empowering the vast majority of people in a high-tech postindustrial society remain under-theorized. Perhaps more than any other recent event, the Great Recession of 2008 has focused considerable public attention on the failures of neoliberal "austerity" policies. Critics argue that the rise of neoliberalism under Prime Minister Thatcher and President Reagan has systematically crippled the necessary steering capacities to mitigate growing social stratification. Francis Fukuyama (2012), for example, argues that there is an acute need for serious intellectual debate with regard to moving beyond neoliberal public policies. As he suggests, there is now a need for a counterrevolutionary ideology to replace neoliberalism:

> Politically, the new ideology would need to reassert the supremacy of democratic politics over economics and legitimate a new government as an expression of the public interest. But the agenda it put forward to protect middle-class life could not simply rely on the existing mechanisms of the welfare state. The ideology would need to somehow redesign the public sector, freeing it from its dependence on existing stakeholders and using new, technology-empowered approaches to delivering services. It would have to argue forthrightly for more redistribution and present a realistic route to ending interest groups' domination of politics. (Fukuyama, 2012, p. 11)

## Beyond the Neoliberal Market State?

At present, this question remains: What counterrevolutionary idea has the wherewithal to displace neoliberalism? Critical scholarship crisscrossing the humanities and social sciences has long challenged neoliberalism as a global policy framework (Jameson, 1984; Lyotard, 1984; Harvey, 2005; Cahil, 2011). Indeed, well before the 2008 financial meltdown, many policy analysts had already recognized the deficiencies of neoliberal economic policy and the limits of financial deregulation (Jenson, 2012, p. 61). Kenworthy (2013), for example, argues that growing poverty, inequality, and economic insecurity demands social democratic welfare policies. Building on theories of endogenous growth, "social investment" thinkers argue that public investments in health care and education are necessary for managing long-term socioeconomic planning. Overlapping the social democratic policies found in the Nordic welfare states, scholars argue that there is room for maximizing both labor force participation and maintaining universal welfare provisions.

Emphasizing human "capacitation," Social Investment Theory views education and lifelong learning as critical to long-run socioeconomic growth (De Deken, 2012, p. 8). In fact, the social investment perspective largely mirrors the kinds of neo-Keynesian social policies advocated by the Obama administration. Rather than a cost and hindrance to economic growth, social investment thinking compares public welfare investments to the fixed capital that supports industrial expansion. Much as the Obama administration has justified its educational reform policies as investments in competitive human capital, so Social Investment Theory makes the claim that welfare policies emphasizing human capacitation can enable more widespread economic prosperity (Morel et al., 2012a).

Contrary to neoliberal policies that curtail social spending on the grounds that public debt undermines economic growth, Social Investment Theory makes the argument that a lack of knowledge-based social investments undermines sustainable innovation. Put differently, increasing the supply of high-quality labor through the provision of welfare services (education, childcare, eldercare, and employment services) enables a broader density of high-value labor and ideas (e.g., European Commission, 2004).

Just as the economic crisis of the 1970s saw the rise of neoliberalism (1970s–1990s) as a replacement for the Keynesian welfare state (1940s–1970s), social investment scholars argue that Social Investment Theory represents a new paradigm for displacing neoliberalism (1990s–present) (table 6.1). Beyond the neoliberal policy dichotomy between

Table 6.1 Models of political economy

|  | Keynesian Paradigm | Neoliberal Paradigm | Social Investment Paradigm |
|---|---|---|---|
| **Unemployment** | Due to insufficient demand | Due to constrained labor supply<br>• Labor market rigidities<br>• High labor costs<br>• Social benefits as work disincentives | Due to lack of adequate skills<br>• STEM Education and Training<br>• Lifelong learning |
| **Social Policy and the Economy** | Positive economic role of social policy<br>• Social insurance props up demand and stimulates growth | Negative economic role of social policy<br>• Welfare state as the cause of slow growth and inflation | Positive economic role of social policy<br>• Social policies are a precondition for growth<br>• Investments support human capital development and labor market fluidity in preparation for KE |
| **Key principles** | • Social equality<br>• Jobs for all (men) | • Individual responsibility<br>• Any job<br>• Activation | • Social inclusion<br>• Knowledge workers<br>• Capacitation |
| **The State** | • Big Welfare state<br>• Central economic planning | • Lean State<br>• Deregulation<br>• Dismantling of the welfare state | • Empowering welfare state<br>• Social policy as long-term planning |
| **Key instruments** | • Policies to support economic demand<br>• Social insurance | • Policies to support supply<br>• Deregulation of the labor market<br>• Privatization of social services | • Human capital investment<br>• Social services and policies to support the labor market |

*Source*: Adapted from Morel et al. (2012b).

economic policy and welfare policy, Social Investment Theory is described as critical to both social and economic development.

Much as theories on endogenous growth, the social investment perspective reaffirms the idea that long-run growth depends upon enduring investments in policy and planning. Put differently, social investment thinkers maintain a belief in the efficacy of the market, but apply a neo-Keynesian approach to steering economic and social outcomes (Morel et al., 2012b, p. 10). Rather than a return to the Keynesian redistribution policy framework of the 1970s (Chenery et al., 1974) however, education and social welfare investments are viewed as key to stimulating long-run socioeconomic development (Esping-Andersen, 1990; Pierson, 2007; Nederveen Pieterse, 2012). Using the language of economics, social investment policy is imagined as having a multiplier effect: increased economic participation for workers provides a positive cycle of increased contributions to the economy. Unlike neoliberal readings of human capital theory, however, this is not merely framed as service to the expansion of corporatized capitalism, but as the enlargement of a country's endogenous capacity for social and economic development. Just as the State mobilizes resources to promote R&D in support of technological innovation (Mazzucato, 2011), the social investment perspective argues that deliberate steps should be taken to deploy scaled investments in promoting human capacitation.

In many ways, the social investment perspective marks a kind of policy synthesis between the welfare focus of Keynesianism and the market focus of neoliberalism. Like neoliberalism, Social Investment Theory focuses on public policy aligned to supply-side economics, but unlike neoliberalism it breaks with any ideological attachment to reducing government. As Hemerijck (2011, p. 14) explains,

> the logic of "social policy as a productive factor" contrasts with neo-classical economics in three crucial dimensions. In the first place, neo-classical economics, based on perfect information and market clearing, theoretically rules out the kind of social risks and market failures that the welfare state seeks to address. Secondly, because neo-classical economics focuses only on the (public) cost side of the welfare state, it is unable to appreciate its core macro- and micro-economic benefits. Thirdly, even where markets function well, collective action problems may obstruct the creation of public goods if participation in the policy cannot be guaranteed and defection is

likely. Markets are destined to undersupply education, the benefits of which cannot be internalised. Extensive comparative empirical research has since the turn of the century revealed that there is no trade-off between macro-economic performance and the size of the welfare state. The presence of a large public sector does not necessarily damage competitiveness. On the contrary, there is a positive relationship between fertility and high levels of female participation in most Scandinavian countries...

Like Keynesianism, social investment emphasizes the role of the State in providing social provisions to maintain socioeconomic growth. In policy terms, this translates as universal investments in lifelong learning, health care, and early childhood care. But where Keynesianism focuses on countercyclical macroeoconomic investments for the here and now, government-driven social investments are framed as public investments for a country's long-term future (Morel et al., 2012a; OECD, 2006).

## Challenges to Social Investment Theory

Despite the important contributions of Social Investment Theory to social policy analysis, there are a number of criticisms that warrant careful consideration. Perhaps the main criticism is that there is no precise definition of "social investment." In fact, critics suggest that Social Investment Theory merely reflects a new phase in the evolution of neoliberalism. Critical literature drawing on Foucault's writing on *governmentality*, point to the inherent "automization and responsibilization" maintained in social investment thinking. Where "spending in areas such as education, childcare and health [are] seen as a *good*... spending on passive welfare such as unemployment benefits [are] seen as *bad*" (Perkins, Nelms, & Smyth, 2004, p. 8). Consequently, "the 'empowerment' of subjects to regulate themselves" remains tightly coupled to the market (Newman, 2001, p. 22).

Where Lundvall (2012) and other social investment scholars highlight the importance of human capital for stoking the "learning economy," one should add the importance of education for meeting the challenge of technological unemployment as well. There is now a wealth of social and economic data demonstrating the correlation between rising unemployment and exponentially advancing technologies. Indeed, the growing literature on labor automation suggests that social investment thinking underestimates both emergent socioeconomic challenges posed by technological innovation, and the very real problem of climate change. Given the rapidly unfolding environmental crisis and its acceleration under neoliberal globalization, it seems simply naive to assume that reforming neoliberalism will be sufficient to counteracting climate change (Klein, 2014).

Bridging the economic and social dimensions of public policy, Social Investment Theory aims to deploy resources that might resolve structural challenges undermining postindustrial societies (i.e., aging populations, changes in family structure, new migration patterns, increased cultural and ethnic diversity). Contemporary arguments in favor of a Basic Minimum Income (BMI), for example, represent policy and planning that complements social investment (Widerquist et al., 2013). But is this sufficient? Are the growing demands for social and political transformation linked to technological innovation and accelerating climate change resolved by simply encouraging more investments in education and social services?

While social policies aimed at front-loading postindustrial societies with the resources to expand knowledge and learning are important, the larger question is whether it's enough to avoid ecological collapse. Developing an alternative to neoliberal public policy is critical to both sustainability and social equity, but is Social Investment Theory sufficient to the task?

## Toward a Knowledge Society

As Marx (1977 [1859]) once wrote, "No social order ever disappears before all the productive forces for which there is room in it have been developed." What has become obvious is that the pace of technological change across sectors of the global economy has made social policy far more daunting (Robinson, 2001; M'Gonigle and Searle, 2006; Christensen et al., 2008). As physical labor has given way to cognitive labor, and manual skills have been superseded by rational and analytical skills, so the value of human capital has risen in correspondence. However, even as technology has boosted economic productivity, it has not ensured rising wages. In fact, over the past decade median incomes have stagnated and even fallen (Brynjolfsson and McAfee, 2011, p. 30).

As Brynjolfsson and McAfee (2014) show, the combined power of digitization, exponential technological change, and recombinant innovation is reconfiguring postindustrial societies and restructuring the logics of market economies. Even if we conservatively assume that engineered machines will never fully displace human labor, it remains the case that our work environments are now being profoundly transformed by computational technologies. For this reason, policymakers will have to begin to rethink the underlying relationship between work and learning.

To put this in perspective, we need to situate these social changes in terms of an emergent "knowledge society." As McNeely and Wolverton (2008) observe, just as older knowledge regimes have been transformed in the past, so today industrial knowledge regimes are being transformed into the future. Much as "libraries spread as agents of empire in ancient times, transplanting Greek culture through the Mediterranean world," so today the Internet has become a foundation for a computational knowledge society.

While industrial civilization has been largely predicated on laboratory science as a knowledge regime, today even this appears to be changing. As a mode of knowledge production, laboratories have transformed industrial societies, splitting the atom, landing human beings on the moon, decoding the structure of DNA, and advancing computing as a new means for producing and consuming innovation itself. However, in the era of network technologies, the laboratory is now being reshaped by the rise of distributed computing. As McNeely and Wolverton suggest, ICTs are producing a network ecology that favors open innovation. Indeed, the Internet's mutualizing capacity may well be the germ of an entirely new open science regime slowly rising to replace the closed ontological spaces of the research laboratory.

What is clear is that while the era of scaled manufacturing favored large corporate enterprises, today the collaborative architecture of ICTs is facilitating highly complex coordination networks. Taken as a whole, these network ecologies are engendering a new cultural modality in which intellectual production is best defined in terms of commons-based peer production. As knowledge itself moves from being a proprietary resource to a shared public good, education is now challenged to develop socially networked structures of knowledge and learning (Cormier, 2010; Bauwens, 2014).

This kind of "public commons" thinking is only bolstered by the affordances of exponential computing. As Rifkin (2014) argues, Moore's law is simultaneously expanding competition while also driving down the costs of production and consumption to near zero. The long-term consequence of this computing revolution is difficult to predict but what it suggests is that societies predicated on trading scarce goods may one day be superseded by complex adaptive societies grounded in supercomputing networks. What remains true (at least for the near term) is that computers will not be able to simulate a process that is not overtly understood by human beings already. But as technology accelerates deep structural change, it is provoking the need for new social and political institutions.

Given the rapid evolution of digital technology and its impact on labor, it seems highly plausible that we are witnessing a long-term transition from a market economy to something else. Notwithstanding the fact that industrial capitalism may subsist as the dominant paradigm of value creation for many decades to come, it remains the case that distributed networks are stimulating a phase transition that is moving us beyond centralized systems.

Bauwens (2012), for example, argues that the scale of this transformation demands a new kind of public administration. In his view, we are witnessing not only the slow death of the neoliberal corporate state but the death of the welfare state as well. Against the backdrop of postindustrialization and growing numbers of precarious knowledge workers, he points to the need for a "Partner State" that might oversee the fixed public capital needed for administering a collaborative commons. Based on the ideas of Italian political scientist Cosma Orsi, the Partner State is conceived as protecting the creation of social value by and for citizens, while at the same time protecting the common infrastructure underlying peer production.

The truth is that our contemporary industrial model of work and learning is simply incompatible with the social and computational ecologies that are remaking our society. As newer methods for managing and producing knowledge displace older methods, so must older institutions and social practices be superseded by newer institutions and practices. Even as US education policy appears hopelessly misaligned with the needs of a computational knowledge economy, there is room for change. Notwithstanding the simplistic and often monolithic conceptions of a knowledge economy, there remain new opportunities for reshaping US social policy.

Responding to the scale of this change is obviously beyond the scope of education. Indeed, it is a complex problem involving a transformation of society as a whole. Beyond the neoliberal market state and its narrow reading of education as human capital formation, policymakers will need to explore new experimental models of education that are informed by pedagogies supporting creativity, entrepreneurship and design. In contrast to learning factories, we now require learning networks that allow individuals and communities to autonomously engage in the practice of building and transforming ideas and artifacts.

This book has been especially focused on deconstructing the discourses that now characterize education policy in the United States. Given the long-term trends toward enhanced computation and automation, it is important to begin to rethink education's role vis-à-vis machine intelligence. At the same time, where modern industrial civilization has been predicated on a machine-like understanding of nature and itself, postindustrial civilization must now embrace an ecological worldview grounded in complex dynamic systems. In the place of an "old story" in which human beings are the masters of a machine-like universe, we now need to cultivate a new story in which we are trustees over our shared social and economic value while at the same time becoming responsible stewards of the Earth.

It is my hope that this book might contribute to US social policy by reframing the debate on education and expanding the discussion on education policy in order to engage with the twenty-first century on its own terms. This includes the development of a proper recognition of the multifaceted nature of KE and the challenges posed by a postindustrial society.

# Notes

## Introduction

1. Put differently, the real cost of computation "has fallen by at least 1.7 trillion-fold since the manual computing era, with most of that decline occurring since 1980" (Autor [2014], *Polanyi's paradox and the shape of employment growth*, NBER working paper no. 20485, retrieved from: http://www.nber.org/papers/w20485, p. 6).
2. The term "postindustrial society" was itself first popularized by Daniel Bell (1973), in *The Coming of Post-industrial Society* (New York: Basic Books) to describe the growing economic importance of knowledge and learning in the context of a service-based economy.

## 1 US Education Policy as Economic Policy

1. Smith wrote, the "improved dexterity of a workman may be considered in the same light as a machine or instrument of trade which facilitates and abridges labor, and which, though it costs a certain expense, repays that expense with a profit."
2. Accordingly, technological innovation is increasing the relative productivity of high-skilled labor making "skill factor bias" pivotal to growing debates around income disparity.
3. Lifelong learning policy is largely a construction of international policy organizations. Beginning in the 1970s, policy proposals introduced by intergovernmental organizations (IGOs) such as the OECD (2004), the European Commission (2003), and the World Bank (2005) began emphasizing for the continuous building of knowledge and skills for the sake of social and economic development.
4. Framing this decline in terms of low-quality education, the report offers five recommendations for reforming education. These include: (1) adding "five new basics" to the school curriculum (four years of English, three years of math, three years of science, three years of social studies, and half a year of computer science in high school); (2) more rigorous and measurable standards

be adopted; (3) an extension of the school year in order to make more time for learning the "New Basics"; (4) teacher improvement through enhanced preparation and professionalization; (5) accountability.
5. In many ways, ANAR was a response to the many "radical" educational reforms introduced in the 1960s and 1970s that were felt to have been responsible for declining educational quality. While reforms stemmed from a desire to advance racial equity and social justice, declining SAT scores in the mid-1970s emboldened many conservatives to focus on the "standards" movement.
6. According to critics, the report was in fact wrong on several counts: "First, it wrongly concluded that student achievement was declining. Second, it placed the blame on schools for national economic problems over which schools have relatively little influence. Third, it ignored the responsibility of the nation's other social and economic institutions for learning" (R. Rothstein, [2008, April 7], "A nation at risk" twenty-five years later, CATO Unbound, retrieved from http://www.cato-unbound.org/2008/04/07/richard-rothstein/nation-risk-twenty-five-years-later).

## 2 THE KNOWLEDGE ECONOMY IN CONTEXT

1. For Touraine (1971), postindustrial society referred to a society focused on the production of "symbolic goods" including the industrialization of all areas of cultural reproduction (health, R&D, education, etc.).
2. For Masuda, KE represented the rise of a new information-driven global consciousness and a "higher stage of social evolution."
3. The paradox of the economic boom across many state capitalist societies is that wealth has largely benefitted a super-elite (P. Dicken, *Global shift: Mapping the changing contours of the world economy* [New York: Guilford Press, 2011], 489–491). Additionally, the extent to which state capitalist economies can generate innovation remains to be seen. What does seem certain, however, is that the "commanding heights" of state capitalism are increasingly dominated by ruling political elites and their families. This is exacerbated by the fact that since 1950, virtually all of the world's population growth (greater than 90%) has occurred in developing countries. Add to this, more than 50 percent of the labor force is employed in the agricultural sector (close to 70% percent in sub-Saharan Africa). Challenges facing BRIC countries are daunting. Together, BRIC countries must provide for more than 40 percent of the world's population. One-third of India's population remains illiterate, and the bulk of China's population is desperately poor. China's cities are among the most polluted in the world today, and the disparity between rich and poor within and between regions is substantial.
4. In many advanced economies, this growing nervousness translates as a politics of anti-immigration and rising calls to reduce or eliminate immigration altogether. This is remarkable given the increasing need for skilled labor across older industrialized economies (especially in Europe and Japan). In the

United States, this is more remarkable still because immigration has been a major source of its substantial economic growth (A. L. Saxenian [2006], *The new argonauts: Regional advantage in a global economy* [Cambridge, MA: Harvard University Press]; Dicken, *Global shift*, 2011).
5. With a combined GDP of $15.4 trillion, the BRIC countries are the four largest economies outside the OECD. As one commentator observes, "Brazil is to agriculture what India is to business offshoring and China to manufacturing: a powerhouse whose size and efficiency few competitors can match" (A. Beattie [2005], Top of the crops: Brazil's huge heartland is yielding farms that can feed the world, *Financial Times*, June 23, p. 17).
6. Roughly equivalent in size to the next three largest economies (China, Japan, and Germany), the United States has a GDP that is larger than France, Brazil, the United Kingdom, Italy, Russia and Canada combined. It accounts for one-fifth of the world's manufacturing, 28 percent of its services, and 8 percent of its agricultural production (Dicken, *Global shift*, 2011).
7. ARPA-E is envisioned as the locus of energy planning and research in the United States.
8. American COMPETES is short for America Creating Opportunities to Meaningfully Promote Excellence in Technology, Education, and Science.
9. Following Marx, Schumpeter argued that technological innovation (rather than price competition) was the underlying driver of capitalist economy (Mazzucato, 2011).
10. The term "Washington Consensus" was first coined in 1990 by the economist John Williamson to describe broad economic policy prescriptions that constituted the "standard" reform package promoted by Washington, DC-based institutions (particularly the IMF and the World Bank). From the 1970s through to the 1990s, the adoption of these policies was generally a precondition to receiving aid.
11. Linking fluid labor markets to income security, B-Å. Lundvall and E. Lorenz (2012) (Social investment in the globalising learning economy: A European perspective, in N. Morel, B. Palier, & J. Palme (Eds.), *Towards a social investment welfare state*. Chicago, IL: Policy Press) argue that flexible labor markets make it possible to continuously reshape the capabilities of knowledge-based societies. They note that a combination of national labor markets that promote high levels of unemployment support alongside relatively low levels of employment protection have an advantage in promoting learning and knowledge exploration across national labor systems (p. 245). In addition to liberalizing the process of hiring and firing, however, Social Investment Theory emphasizes State support in education and training to ensure a consistent proliferation of knowledge and skills (p. 253).

## 3 Paradigms of the Knowledge Economy

1. From an analytical standpoint, discussions on peer production overlap much broader research on complexity and complex systems. Central to a complexity

approach is the idea that learning emerges from collective activity. In his 1998 book *Complexity and postmodernism: Understanding complex systems* (London: Routledge), Paul Cilliers defines complexity this way:

> In a complex system... the interaction constituents of the system, and the interaction between the system and its environment, are of such a nature that the system as a whole cannot be fully understood simply by analysing its components. Moreover, these relationships are not fixed, but shift and change, often as a result of self-organisation. This can result in novel features, usually referred to in terms of emergent properties. (p. viii)

Self-organization is an emergent property of the system as a whole, enabling it "to develop or change internal structure spontaneously and adaptively in order to cope with or manipulate the environment" Cilliers (1998, p. 90). Much as other complex systems, network production systems avoid creative entropy by continually absorbing energy and resources from new participants. By "importing" energy across permeable boundaries, complex systems are able to continually absorb the resources needed for growth. It is this capacity for self-creation or autopoesis that gives complex systems their incredible resilience (P. Haynes [2007], *Complexity theory and evaluation in public management: A qualitative approach* [Health and Public Policy Research Centre, University of Brighton]). When this same boundary permeability is translated into the domain of networked social production, it manifests as a continually evolving "collective intelligence" (P. Lévy [1997], *Collective intelligence: Mankind's emerging world in cyberspace* [New York: Plenium]).

2. Hesmondhalgh and Pratt trace the manner in which the term "culture" has been expanded far beyond its original meaning. As they write, "Some have argued, on the basis of the flexibility of the term culture, that it is useless to talk of the cultural activities at all. Others have also implied this by arguing that all industries are cultural, because all industries are involved in the production of goods and services which become part of the web of meaning we know as culture" (D. Hesmondhalgh & A. C. Pratt [2005], Cultural industries and cultural policy, *International Journal of Cultural Policy*, *11*(1), 6).

# 4 Education Policy and the Obama Administration

1. Flying in the face of neoclassical economic theory, the scale of the financial and economic disaster facing the United States and other advanced capitalist countries justified mammoth stimulus spending. Notwithstanding this massive spending, both political parties have historically supported countercyclical stimulus policy.
2. This included federal tax cuts ($288 billion); expansion of unemployment benefits ($82.5 billion); social welfare and domestic spending including education ($90 billion), health care ($147.7 billion), and infrastructure ($80.9

billion); and investments in the energy sector ($61.3 billion), housing ($12.7 billion), scientific research ($8.9 billion), and other projects ($18.1 billion).
3. Title I was intended to close the skill gap in reading, writing, and mathematics between low-income urban and rural students and higher-income suburban students.
4. Roughly paralleling the structure of *A Blueprint for Reform*, the six reports included: (1) college- and career-ready students; (2) great teachers and great leaders; (3) meeting the needs of english language learners and other diverse learners; (4) a complete education; (5) successful, safe and healthy schools; 6) fostering innovation and excellence.
5. Highlighting the *Higher Education Opportunity Act* (P. L. 110–315), passed in August 2008, and the introduction of the National Center for Research in Advanced Information and Digital Technologies (or Digital Promise), the authors highlight the potential of "grand challenge problems" to incentivize communities of scientists and researchers to build solutions for education.

## 5  THE KNOWLEDGE ECONOMY IN DIALOGUE

1. His writing in *The Social Contract* (1762) and *Émile: or, On Education* (1762) form the philosophical underpinnings and intellectual tributaries for contemporary notions of developmental learning.

## 6  RETHINKING US EDUCATION POLICY

1. Informatics combines "information" with "automation" in the interactions between human beings and digital technologies. Where computer science is focused on the design of hardware and software, informatics emphasizes the intersection of people, information, and technological systems.

# Bibliography

Acemoglu, D., & Autor, D. (2012). What does human capital do? A review of Goldin and Katz's *The race between education and technology*. *Journal of Economic Literature, 50*(2), 426–463.
Adorno, T., & Horkheimer, M. (1944/1977). Culture industry: Enlightenment as mass deception. In J. Curran, M. Gurevitch, & J. Woolacott (Eds.), *Mass communication and society* (pp. 349–383). London: Arnold/Open University.
Apple, M. W. (2006). *Educating the "right" way: Markets, standards, God and inequality*. New York: Routledge.
Araya, D. (2011). Collective intelligence. In D. Araya, Y. Breindl, & T. Houghton (Eds.), *Nexus: New intersections in Internet research*. New York: Peter Lang.
Araya, D., & Peters, M. (2010). *Education in the creative economy: Knowledge and learning in the age of innovation*. New York: Peter Lang.
Araya, D. (2013). Towards post-industrial education: State capitalism and China. In D. Araya & P. Marber (Eds.), *Higher education in the global age: Policy, practice, and promise in emerging societies*. New York: Routledge.
Araya, D., & Marber, P. (Eds.) (2013). *Higher education in the global age: Policy, practice, and promise in emerging societies*. New York: Routledge.
Aronowitz, S. (2000). *The knowledge factory: Dismantling the corporate university and creating true higher learning*. Boston, MA: Beacon Press.
Atkins, D., Bennett, J., Brown, S. J., Dede, C., Fishman, B., Means, B., Pea, R., Thill, C. & Williams, B. (2011). Response to the articles on draft 2010: National educational technology plan. *E-Learning and Digital Media, 8*(2), 170–174.
Autor, D., Levy, F., & Murnane, R. (2003). The skill content of recent technological change: An empirical exploration. *Quarterly Journal of Economics, 118*(4), 1279–1333.
Autor, D. (2014). *Polanyi's paradox and the shape of employment growth*. NBER Working paper no. 20485. Retrieved from http://www.nber.org/papers/w20485.
Ball, S. (2006). *Education policy and social class: The selected works of Stephen J. Ball*. London: Routledge.
Barabási, A. L. (2002). *Linked: The new science of networks*. Cambridge, MA: Perseus Publishing.
Barbrook, R. (2006). *The class of the new*. London: OpenMute.
Barton, P. E. (2005). One-third of a nation: Rising drop-out rates and declining opportunities. *Educational Testing Services, Policy Information Center*. Retrieved from http://www.ets.org/Media/Education_Topics/pdf/onethird.pdf.

Bauer, J. M. (2012). Entrepreneurship and government in U.S. high-tech policy. In J. M. Bauer, A. Lang, & V. Schneider (Eds.), *Innovation policies and governance in high-technology industries: The complexity of coordination* (pp. 103–125). Berlin: Springer.

Bauwens, M. (2009). Class and capital in peer production. *Capital & Class, 33*(97), 121–141.

Bauwens, M. (2014, April). Beyond Jeremy Rifkin: How will the phase transition to a commons economy actually occur? *Huffington Post.* Retrieved from http://www.huffingtonpost.com/michel-bauwens/beyond-jeremy-rifkin-how-_b_5185948.html.

Beattie, A. (2005). Top of the crops: Brazil's huge heartland is yielding farms that can feed the world. *Financial Times,* June 23, p. 17.

Becker, G. (1964). *Human capital.* Chicago: University of Chicago Press.

Becker, G. (1975). *Human capital: A theoretical and empirical analysis, with special reference to education.* New York: Columbia University Press.

Bekman, E., Bound, J., & Machin, S. (1998). Implications of skill-biased technological change: International evidence. *Quarterly Journal of Economics, 113*(4), 1245–1279.

Bell, D. (1973). *The coming of post-industrial society.* New York: Basic Books.

Beniger, J. R. (1986). *The control revolution: Technological and economic origins of the information society.* Cambridge, MA: Harvard University Press.

Benkler, Y. (2006). *The wealth of networks: How social production transforms markets and freedom.* Princeton, NJ: Princeton University Press.

Bernstein, J., & Mishel, L. (2007). Economy's gains fail to reach most workers' paychecks. EPI Briefing paper no. 195. Washington, DC: Economic Policy Institute.

Bereiter, C. (2002). Education in a knowledge society. In B. Smith (Ed.), *Liberal education in a knowledge society.* Chicago: Open Court. Retrieved from http://www.ikit.org/fulltext/inpresseducation.pdf.

Bereiter, C. (2002b). *Education and mind in the knowledge age.* Mahwah, NJ: Lawrence Erlbaum Associates.

Bergson, H. (1944). *Creative evolution.* A. Mitchell (Trans.). New York: Modern Library.

Berry, C., & Glaeser, E. L. (2005). The divergence of human capital levels across cities. *Regional Science, 84*(3), 407–444.

Blair, T., & Shroeder, G. (1998). Europe: The third way. Retrieved from http://library.fes.de/pdf-files/bueros/suedafrika/02828.pdf.

Blinder, A. S. (2008). Education for the third industrial revolution. Working paper 1047, Center for Economic Policy Studies, Department of Economics, Princeton University. Retrieved from http://www.princeton.edu/ceps/workingpapers/163blinder.pdf.

Bourdieu, P. (1972). *Outline of a theory of practice.* Cambridge: Cambridge University Press.

Bourdieu, P. (1986). The forms of capital. In J. G. Richardson (Ed.), *Handbook of theory and research for the sociology of education* (pp. 241–258). New York: Greenwood Press.

Bourdieu, P. (1998). The myth of "globalization" and the European welfare state. In *Acts of resistance: Against the tyranny of the market* (pp. 29–44). New York: New Press.

Bowles, S., & Gintis, H. (1976). *Schooling in capitalist America: Education reform and the contradictions of economic Life*. New York: Basic Books

Brand, U. (2012). Green economy—the next oxymoron? No lessons learned from failures of implementing sustainable development. *GAIA, 21*(1), 28–32.

Brown, J. S., & Adler, R. P. (2008, January/February). Minds on fire: Open education, the long tail, and learning 2.0. *EDUCAUSE Review*.

Brown, J. S., Collins, A., & Duguid, S. (1989). Situated cognition and the culture of learning. *Educational Researcher, 18*(1), 32–42.

Brown, P., Lauder, H., & Ashton, D. (2010). *The global auction: The broken promises of education, jobs, and rewards*. New York: Oxford University Press.

Brynjolfsson, E., & McAfee, A. (2011). *Race against the machine: How the digital revolution is accelerating innovation, driving productivity, and irreversibly transforming employment and the economy*. New York: Digital Frontier Press.

Brynjolfsson, E., & McAfee, A. (2014). *The second machine age: Work, progress, and prosperity in a time of brilliant technologies*. New York: W. W. Norton.

Bureau of Labor Statistics. (2011, August 24). Employment and unemployment among youth summary. Retrieved from http://www.bls.gov/news.release/youth.nr0.htm.

Bureau of Labor Statistics. (2014, June 9). Labor force statistics from the current population survey. Retrieved from http://data.bls.gov/timeseries/LNU01300000.

Burton-Jones, A. (1999). *Knowledge capitalism: Business, work, and learning in the new Economy*. Oxford: Oxford University Press.

Bruns, A. (2008). *Blogs, wikipedia, second life, and beyond: From production to produsage*. New York: Peter Lang.

Cahil, D. (2011). Beyond neoliberalism? Crisis and the prospects for progressive alternatives. *New Political Science, 33*(4), 479–492.

Campbell, T. (2012). *Beyond smart cities: How cities network, learn, and innovate*. New York: Earthscan.

Castells, M. (2000). *The rise of the networked society*. Oxford: Blackwell.

Cerny, P. (1990). *The changing architecture of politics: Structure, agency and the future of the state*. London: Sage.

Chenery, H., Ahluwalia, M., Bell, C., Duloy, J., & Jolly, R. (1974). *Redistribution and growth*. Oxford: Oxford University Press for the World Bank.

Chiu, R. (2012). *Entrepreneurship education in the Nordic countries: Strategy implementation and good practice*. Oslo: Nordic Innovation Publication.

Christensen, C. M. (1997). *The innovator's dilemma: When new technologies cause great firms to fail*. Boston, MA: Harvard Business School Press.

Christensen, C. M., Horn, M. B., & Johnson, C. W. (2008). *Disrupting class: How disruptive innovation will change the way the world learns*. New York: McGraw Hill.

Cilliers, P. (1998). *Complexity and postmodernism: Understanding complex systems*. London: Routledge.

Cimoli, M., Dosi, G., & Stiglitz, J. (2009). *The political economy of capabilities accumulation: The past and future of policies for industrial development*. Oxford: Oxford University Press.

Collins, J. W., & Weiner, S. A. (2010). Proposal for the creation of a subdiscipline: Education informatics. *Teachers College Record, 112*(10), 2523–2536. Retrieved from http://www.tcrecord.org/Content.asp?ContentID=15867.
Cormier, D. (2010). Community as curriculum. In D. Araya & M. A. Peters (Eds.), *Education in the creative economy*. New York: Peter Lang.
Cormier, D. (2008). Rhizomatic education: Community as curriculum. Retrieved from http://davecormier.com/edblog/2008/06/03/rhizomatic-education-community-as-curriculum/.
Cowen, T. (2011). *The great stagnation: How America ate all the low-hanging fruit of modern history, got sick, and will (eventually) feel better*. New York: Dutton.
Cozzens, S. (2011). End of empire: External and internal transitions in US policies for science, technology and innovation. *Prometheus: Critical Studies in Innovation, 29*(4), 393–409.
Cunningham, S. (2001). From cultural to creative industries, theory, industry and policy implications. *Culturelink*, Special Issue, 19–32.
Daly, H. (1996). *Beyond growth: The economics of sustainable development*. Boston, MA: Beacon Press.
Daly, H., & Farley, J. (2010). *Ecological economics: Principles and applications* (2nd ed.). Washington, DC: Island Press.
Darling-Hammond, L. (2010). *The flat world and education*. New York: Teachers College Press.
Davidson, C., & Goldberg, D. (2010). *The future of thinking: Learning institutions in a digital age*. Cambridge, MA: MIT Press.
Dede, C. (2013). Opportunities and challenges for educational transformation via learning technologies. In J. Guthrie (Ed.), *A bigger bang for education's bucks: Schools America must have at costs America can afford*. Dallas, TX: George W. Bush Institute.
Dewey, J. (1938). *Experience and education*. New York: Kappa Delta Pi.
Dewey, J. (1991 [1940]). Creative Democracy—The Task Before Us. In J. A. Boydston (Ed.), *John Dewey: The Later Works* (vol. 14). Carbondale: Southern Illinois University Press.
Dewey, J. (2008). *Democracy and education*. Radford, VA: Wilder.
De Deken, J. (2012). Identifying the skeleton of the social investment state: Defining and measuring patterns of social policy change on the basis of expenditure data. Presented at ESPANET 2012 Conference Edinburgh, Scotland, September 6–8, 2012.
De Long, J. B. (1998). What 'new' economy? *Wilson Quarterly, 22*(4), pp. 14–26.
Delors, J. (1996). Learning: The treasure within Report to UNESCO of the International Commission on Education for the Twenty-first Century. Paris: UNESCO. Retrieved from http://plato.acadiau.ca/courses/pols/conley/QUEBEC98/DELORS-1/delors_e.pdf.
Dicken, P. (2011). *Global shift: Mapping the changing contours of the world economy*. New York: Guilford Press.
Dobrowolsky, A. (2002). Rhetoric versus reality: The figure of the child and New Labour's "strategic social investment state." *Studies in political economy, 69*, 43–74.

Drucker, P. (1969). *The age of discontinuity: Guidelines to our changing society*. New York: Harper & Row.
Drucker, P. (1994). *Post-Capitalist society*. New York: HarperBusiness.
Duncan, A. (2009). Speech at the national press club. Retrieved from http://www.ed.gov/news/speeches/quiet-revolution-secretary-arne-duncans-remarks-national-press-club.
Dyer-Witheford, N. (2000). *Cyber-Marx: Cycles and circuits of struggle in high-technology capitalism*. Chicago: University of Illinois Press.
*Economist*. (2013a). The gated globe: Governments are putting up impediments to globalisation. It is time for a fresh wave of liberalisation. Retrieved from http://www.economist.com/news/leaders/21587785-gated-globe.
*Economist*. (2013b, November 7). On your marks: States are starting to test teachers. Retrieved from http://www.economist.com/news/united-states/21589427-states-are-starting-test-teachers-your-marks.
*Economist*. (2014). Coming to an office near you: The effect of today's technology on tomorrow's jobs will be immense—and no country is ready for it. Retrieved from http://www.economist.com/news/leaders/21594298-effect-todays-technology-tomorrows-jobs-will-be-immenseand-no-country-ready.
Engebart, D. C. (1962). *Augmenting human intellect: A conceptual framework*. Summary report AFOSR-3223, Stanford Research Institute, Menlo Park, CA.
Esping-Andersen, G. (1990). *The three worlds of welfare capitalism*. Cambridge: Polity Press.
Esping-Andersen, G. (1996). After the golden age? Welfare state dilemmas in a global economy. In G. Esping-Andersen (Ed.), *Welfare states in transition: National adaptations in global economies* (pp. 1–31). London: UNRISD.
Esping-Andersen, G., Gallie, D., Hemerijck, A., & Myles, J. (2002). *Why we need a new welfare state*. Oxford: Oxford University Press.
European Commission. (2004). Report of the High Level Group on the future of social policy in an enlarged European Union, Report of the High Level Group. Retrieved from http://www.pedz.uni-mannheim.de/daten/edz-fd/gds/hlg_social_elarg_en.pdf.
Featherstone, B. (2006). Rethinking family support in the current policy context. *British Journal of Social Work, 36*, 5–19.
Florida, R. (2002a). *The rise of the creative class: And how it's transforming work, leisure, community and everyday life*. New York: Basic Books.
Florida, R. (2002b). The Economic Geography of Talent. *Annals of the Association of American Geographers, 92*(4), 743–755.
Florida, R. (2005a). *Cities and the creative class*. New York: Routledge.
Florida, R. (2005b, October). "The world is spiky." *Atlantic Monthly*. Retrieved from http://www.theatlantic.com/past/docs/images/issues/200510/world-is-spiky.pdf.
Florida, R. (2007). *The flight of the creative class: The new global competition for talent*. New York: HarperCollins.
Florida, R. (2011). *The great reset: How the post-crash economy will change the way we live and work*. New York: HarperBusiness.
Foray, D. (2004). *Economics of knowledge*. Cambridge, MA: MIT Press.

Foucault, M. (1977). *The archeology of knowledge*. London: Tavistock.
Freeman, C. (1987). *Technology and economic performance: Lessons from Japan*. London: Pinter.
Freeman, C. (1995). The National System of Innovation in Historical Perspective. *Cambridge Journal of Economics, 19*(1), 5–24.
Freeman, C., & Soete, L. (1997). *The economics of industrial innovation*. New York: Routledge.
Freeman, R. (2012, May). Toward economic feudalism? Inequality, financialisation, and democracy. LSE Lecture. Retrieved from http://www2.lse.ac.uk/newsAndMedia/videoAndAudio/channels/publicLecturesAndEvents/player.aspx?id=1457.
Frey, C. B., & Osborne, M. A. (2013). The future of employment: How susceptible are jobs to computerisation? Retrieved from http://www.futuretech.ox.ac.uk/sites/futuretech.ox.ac.uk/files/The_Future_of_Employment_OMS_Working_Paper_1.pdf.
Freire, P. (1970). *Pedagogy of the oppressed*. Myra Bergman Ramos (Trans.). New York: Herder and Herder.
Friedlaender, D., & Darling-Hammond, L. (2007). High schools for equity: Policy supports for student learning in communities of color. Retrieved from http://www.justicematters.org/jmi_live/jmi_sec/jmi_dwnlds/hsfe_policy_report.pdf.
Friedman, M. (1962). *Capitalism and freedom*. Chicago: University of Chicago Press.
Friedman, T. (2005). *The world is flat: A brief history of the twenty-first century*. New York: Farrar, Straus and.
Fuchs, C. (2008). *Internet and society: Social theory in the information age*. New York: Routledge.
Fukuyama, F. (2012, January). The future of history: Can liberal democracy survive the decline of the middle class? *Foreign Affairs*. Retrieved from http://www.foreignaffairs.com/articles/136782/francis-fukuyama/the-future-of-history>.
Galloway, S., & Dunlop, S. (2007). A critique of definitions of the cultural and creative industries in public policy. *International Journal of Cultural Policy, 13*(1), 17–31.
Garrison, J. (2012). Individuality, equality, and creative democracy—the task before us. *American Journal of Education, 118*(3), 369–379.
Gardner, H. (1983). *Frames of mind: The theory of multiple intelligences*. New York: Basic Books.
Ghose, A. K., Majid, N., & Ernst, C. (2009). *The global employment challenge*. Geneva: ILO.
Gibb, A. (2002). In pursuit of a new "enterprise" and "entrepreneurship" paradigm for learning: Creative destruction, new values, new ways of doing things and new combinations of knowledge. *International Journal of Management Reviews, 4*(3), 233–269.
Giddens, A. (1998). *The third way: The renewal of social democracy*. Cambridge: Polity Press.
Giroux, H. A. (2001). Critical education or training: Beyond the commodification of higher education. In H. A. Giroux & K. Myrsiades (Eds.), *Beyond the*

*corporate university culture and pedagogy in the new millennium* (pp. 1–13). Lanham, MD: Rowman & Littlefield.
Giroux, H. A. (2003). Critical theory and educational practice. In A. Darder, M. Baltodano, & R. D. Torres (Eds.), *The critical pedagogy reader* (pp. 27–56). New York: RoutledgeFarmer.
Godofsky, J., Zikin, C., & Horn, C.V. (2011). *Unfulfilled expectations: Recent college graduates struggle in a troubled economy*. New Brunswick, NJ: John J. Heldrich Center for Workforce Development, Rutgers University.
Goldin, C., & Katz, L. F. (2008). *The race between education and technology*. Cambridge, MA: Harvard University Press.
Granovetter, M. S. (1973). The strength of weak ties. *American Journal of Sociology*, *78*(60), 1360–1380.
Gross, D. (2007, January 28). The U.S. is losing market share. So what? *The New York Times*. Retrieved from http://www.nytimes.com/2007/01/28/business/yourmoney/28view.html?fta=y.
Hall, P. (1993). Policy paradigm, social learning, and the state. *Comparative Politics*, *25*(3), 275–296.
Hall, P. A., & Soskice, D. (Eds.). (2001). *Varieties of capitalism: The institutional foundations of comparative advantage*. Oxford: Oxford University Press, 2001.
Hardt, M., & Negri, A. (2000). *Empire*. Cambridge, MA: Harvard University Press.
Hardt, M., & Negri, A. (2009). *Commonwealth*. Cambridge, MA: Harvard University Press.
Hartley, J. (Ed.). (2005). *The creative industries*. New York: Wiley-Blackwell.
Harvey, D. (2005). *A brief history of neoliberalism*. New York: Oxford University Press.
Hayek, F. A. (1937). Economics and knowledge. *Economica*, *4*(13), 33–54.
Hayek, F. A. (1944). *The road to serfdom*. Chicago: University of Chicago Press.
Hayek, F. A. (1960). *The constitution of liberty*. Chicago: University of Chicago Press.
Haynes, P. (2007). *Complexity theory and evaluation in public management: A qualitative approach*. Health and Public Policy Research Centre, University of Brighton.
Hearn, G. and Rooney, D. (Eds.) (2008). *Knowledge policy: Challenges for the 21st century*. Cheltenham: Edward Elgar.
Hemerijck, A. (2011). The social investment imperative beyond the financial crisis. *Challenge Europe*. Brussels: European Policy Centre, pp. 11–19.
Hemerijck, A. (2012). Two or three waves of welfare state transformation? In N. Morel, B. Palier, & J. Palme (Eds.), *Towards a social investment welfare state: Ideas, policies and challenges*. Chicago, IL: Policy Press.
Hesmondhalgh, D. (2002). *The cultural industries*. London: Sage.
Hesmondhalgh, D., & Pratt, A. C. (2005). Cultural industries and cultural policy. *International Journal of Cultural Policy*, *11*(1), 1–13.
Hilton, J., Wiley, D., Stein, J., & Johnson, A. (2010). The four R's of openness and ALMS Analysis: Frameworks for Open Educational Resources. *Open Learning: The Journal of Open and Distance Learning*, *25*(1), 37–44.
Hobsbawm, E. (2009, April 10). Socialism has failed. Now capitalism is bankrupt. So what comes next? *The Guardian*. Retrieved from http://www.theguardian.com/commentisfree/2009/apr/10/financial-crisis-capitalism-socialism-alternatives.

Hollands, R. (2008). Will the real smart city stand up? Creative, progressive, or just entrepreneurial? *City 12*(3), 303–320.

Horkheimer, M., & Adorno, T. (2002). *Dialectic of enlightenment*. Stanford, CA: Stanford University Press.

Horn, M. B., & Mackey, (2011). Transforming American education. *E-Learning and Digital Media 8*(2), 133–144.

Howkins, J. (2001). *The creative economy: How people make money from ideas*. London: Allen Lane.

Iiyoshi, T., & Kumar, M. S. V. (Eds.). (2010). *Opening up education: The collective advancement of education through open technology, open content and open knowledge*. Cambridge, MA: MIT Press.

ILO. (2009). The green jobs program of the ILO. Retrieved from: http://www.ilo.org/public/libdoc/ilo/2009/447728.pdf.

Ito, M., Horst, H., Bittanti, M., Boyd, D., Herr-Stephenson, B., Lange, P.,...Robinson, L. (2008). *Living and learning with new media: Summary of Findings from the digital youth project*. The John D. and Catherine T. MacArthur Foundation Reports on Digital Media and Learning. Cambridge, MA: MIT Press.

Jenson, J. (2010). Diffusing ideas for after neoliberalism: The social investment perspective in Europe and Latin America. *Global Social Policy, 10*(1), 59–84.

Jenson, J. (2012). Redesigning citizenship regimes after neoliberalism: Moving towards social investment. In N. Morel, B. Palier, & J. Palme (Eds.), *Towards a social investment welfare state*. Chicago, IL: Policy Press.

Jenson, J., & Saint-Martin, D. (2003). New Routes to Social Cohesion? Citizenship and the Social Investment State. *Canadian Journal of Sociology, 28*(1), 77–99.

Jones, V. (2008). *The green-collar economy: How one solution can fix our two biggest problems*. New York: HarperOne.

Katz, L. (1999). Technological change, computerization, and the wage structure. Department of Economics, Harvard University. Retrieved from http://scholar.harvard.edu/files/lkatz/files/technological_change_computerization_and_the_wage_structure.pdf.

Kelty, C. (2008). *Two bits: The cultural significance of free software*. Durham: Duke University Press.

Kenway, J., Bullen, E., Fahey, J., & Robb, S. (2006). *Haunting the knowledge economy*. New York: Routledge.

Kenworthy, L. (2013). *Social democratic America*. New York: Oxford University Press.

Kenworthy, L. (2014). America's social democratic future: The arc of policy is long but bends toward justice. *Foreign Affairs, 93*(1), 86–100.

Kerr, C. (1963). *The uses of the university*. Cambridge: Harvard University Press.

Klein, N. (2014). *This changes everything: Capitalism vs. the climate*. New York: Simon & Shuster.

Kohlberg, L. (1969). Stage and sequence: The cognitive developmental approach to socialization. In D. Goslin (Ed.), *Handbook of socialization*: *Theory and research*. New York: Rand McNally.

Kuhn, T. (1962). *The structure of scientific revolutions*. Chicago, IL: University of Chicago Press.

Kumashiro, K. K. (2012). Reflections on "bad teachers." *Berkeley Review of Education*, *3*(1), 5–16.
Kurzweil, R. (2006). *The singularity is near: When humans transcend biology*. New York: Penguin Books.
Ladson-Billings, G. (2006). From the achievement gap to the education debt: Understanding achievement in U.S. schools. *Educational Researcher*, *35*(7), 3–12.
Laloux, F. (2014). *Reinventing organizations: A guide to creating organizations inspired by the next stage of human consciousness*. Brussels: Nelson Parker.
Lander, E. (2011). The green economy: A wolf in sheep's clothing. Retrieved from http://www.tni.org/report/green-economy-wolf-sheeps-clothing.
Landry, C. (2000). *The creative city: A toolkit for urban innovators*. London: Earthscan.
Lauder, H., Brown, P., & Ashton, D. (2008). Education, globalization and skill. In G. McCulloch & D. Crook (Eds.), *The Routledge International Encyclopedia of Education*. Routledge.
Lave, J. (1988). *Cognition in practice*. Cambridge, UK: Cambridge University Press.
Lave J., & Wenger E. (1991). *Situated learning: Legitimate peripheral participation*. New York: Cambridge University Press.
Leadbeater, C. (2000). *Living on thin air: The new economy*. London: Penguin.
Leadbeater, C., & Miller, P. (2004). *The pro-am revolution: How enthusiasts are changing our economy and society*. London: Demos.
Lessig, L. (2004). *Free culture: How big media uses technology and the law to lock down culture and control creativity*. New York: Penguin.
Lévy, P. (1997). *Collective intelligence: Mankind's emerging world in cyberspace*. New York: Plenium.
Lin, J. Y., & Chang, H-J. (2009). DPR Debate: Should Industrial Policy in Developing Countries Conform to Comparative Advantage or Defy It? *Development Policy Review*, *27*(5), 483–502.
Lin, J., & Monga, C. (2011). *Growth identification and facilitation: The role of the state in the dynamics of structural change*. World Bank Policy Research Working Paper 5313. Washington, DC: World Bank.
Lipman, P. (2009). *The new political economy of urban education: Neoliberalism, race, and the right to the city*. New York: Routledge.
Lipman, P. (2011). Education and the right to the city: The intersection of urban policies, education, and poverty. In M. Apple, L. Armand Gandin, & S. Ball (Eds.), *International Handbook of the Sociology of Education*. London: Routledge.
List, F. (1909.) *The national system of political economy*. London: Longmans Green.
Lister, R. (2003). Investing in the citizen-workers of the future: Transformations in citizenship and the state under new labour. *Social Policy & Administration*, *37*(5), 427–443.
Longworth, N., & Davies, K. (1996). *Lifelong learning: New vision, new implications, new roles for people, organizations, nations and communities in the 21st century*. London: Kogan Page.
Lorenz, E. and Lundvall, B-A. (Eds.) (2006). *How Europe's economies learn*. Oxford: Oxford University Press.
Lucas, R. (1988). On the mechanics of economic development. *Journal of Monetary Economics*, *22*(1), pp. 3–42.

Lundvall, B-Å. (2004). *Why the New Economy is a Learning Economy*. DRUID, Aalborg University. (DRUID Working Paper Series; No. 04–01).
Lundvall, B-Å. (Ed.). (1992). *National innovation systems: Towards a theory of innovation and interactive learning*. London: Pinter.
Lundvall, B-Å., & Johnson, B. (1994). The learning economy. *Journal of Industry Studies, 1*(2), 23–42.
Lundvall, B-Å., & Lorenz, E. (2012). Social investment in the globalising learning economy: A European perspective. In N. Morel, B. Palier, & J. Palme (Eds.), *Towards a social investment welfare state*. Chicago, IL: Policy Press.
Lyle, J. T. (1994). *Regenerative design for sustainable development*. New York: John Wiley.
Lyotard, J. (1984). *The post-modern condition: A report on knowledge*. G. Bennington & B. Massumi (Trans.). Minneapolis: University of Minnesota Press.
Marber, P. (2014). *Brave new math: Information, globalization and the need for new policy thinking in the 21st Century*. New York: World Policy.
M'Gonigle, M., & Searle, J. (2006). *Planet U: Sustaining the world, reinventing the university*. Gabriola Island, BC: New Society.
McDonnell, L. M., & Weatherford, M.S. (2011). Crafting an education reform agenda through economic stimulus policy. *Peabody Journal of Education, 86*, 304–318.
McLaren, P. (2007). Critical pedagogy and class struggle in the age of neoliberal globalization: Notes from history's underside. In E. W. Ross & R. Gibson (Eds.), *Neoliberalism and education reform* (pp. 257–288). Cresskill, NJ: Hampton Press.
McMartin, F. (2008). Open educational content: Transforming access to education. In T. Iiyoshi & M. S. V. Kumar (Eds.), *Opening up education*. Cambridge, MA: MIT Press.
McMurtry, J. (1999). *The cancer stage of capitalism*. London: Pluto.
McNeely, I. F., & Wolverton, L. (2008). *Reinventing knowledge: From Alexandria to the Internet*. New York: W. W. Norton.
Machlup, F. (1962). *The production and distribution of knowledge in the United States* Princeton, NJ: Princeton University Press.
Mandel, B. R. (2012). Why is the U.S. share of world merchandise exports shrinking? *Current Issues in Economics and Finance, 18*(1). Retrieved from http://www.newyorkfed.org/research/current_issues/ci18-1.pdf.
Marber, P. (2013). Higher education and emerging markets. In D. Araya & P. Marber, *Higher education in the global age*. New York: Routledge.
Marber, P. (2014). *Brave new math: Information, globalization and the need for new policy thinking in the 21st Century*. New York: Wiley.
Marx, K. (1968 [1848]). *The manifesto of the communist party*. Moscow: Progress.
Marx, K. (1973). *Grundrisse: Foundations of the critique of political economy*. New York: Vintage Books.
Marx, K. (1977 [1859]). *Contribution to the critique of political economy*. Moscow: Progress.
Masuda, Y. (1968). *An introduction to information society*. Tokyo: Pelikan-sha.
Masuda, Y. (1980). *The information society*. Washington, DC: World Future Society.
Mathis, W. J., & Welner, K. G. (Eds.). (2010). *The Obama education blueprint: Researchers examine the evidence*. Charlotte, NC: Information Age Publishers.

Mazzucato, M. (2011). *The entrepreneurial state*. London: Demos.
Mazzucato, M. (2012, September). Public money spent on "digging ditches" won't stimulate the economy. *The Guardian*. Retrieved from http://www.guardian.co.uk/commentisfree/2012/sep/02/state-spending-digging-ditches-transform-economy.
Means, A. (2011). Creativity as an educational problematic within the biopolitical economy. In M. A. Peters & E. Bulut (2011), *Cognitive capitalism, education and digital labor*. New York: Peter Lang.
Mellander, C., & Florida, R. (2007). *The creative class or human capital: Explaining regional development in Sweden*. Stockholm: Royal Institute of Technology. Retrieved from http://www.kth.se/dokument/itm/cesis/CESISWP79.pdf.
Metcalfe, S. (1995). The economic foundations of technology policy: Equilibrium and evolutionary perspectives. In P. Stoneman (Ed.), *Handbook of the economics of innovation and technological change*. Oxford: Blackwell.
Milani, B. (2000). *Designing the green economy: The postindustrial alternative to corporate globalization*. Oxford: Rowman and Littlefield.
Mincer, J. (1958). Investment in Human Capital and Personal Income Distribution. *Journal of Political Economy*, 66(28), 1–302.
Montessori, M. (1964). *The montessori method*. New York: Schocken Books.
Moravec, H. (1988). *Mind children: The future of robot and human intelligence*. Cambridge, MA: Harvard.
Morel, N., Palier, B., & Palme, J. (Eds.) (2012a). *Towards a social investment welfare state: Ideas, policies and challenges*. Chicago, IL: The Policy Press
Morel, N., Palier, B., & Palme, J. (Eds.). (2012b). Beyond the welfare state as we knew it? *Towards a social investment welfare state: Ideas, policies and challenges*. Chicago, IL: Policy Press
Myrdal, A., & Myrdal, G. (1934). *Kris I Befolkningsfragan*. Stockholm: Albert Bonniers Forlag.
National Center for Education Statistics. (2011). *Achievement gaps: How Hispanic and White students in public schools perform in mathematics and reading on the National Assessment of Educational Progress* (NCES document no. 2011485). Washington, DC: National Center for Education Statistics, Institute of Education Studies, US Department of Education. Retrieved from http://nces.ed.gov/nationsreportcard/pdf/studies/2011485.pdf.
National Commission on Excellence in Education. (1983). *A Nation at Risk: The Imperative for Educational Reform*. Report to the nation and the secretary of education, April. Washington, DC: US Department of Education.
National Intelligence Council. (2012). *Global trends 2030: Alternative worlds*. Washington DC: US National Intelligence Council.
Nederveen Pieterse, J. (2010). Innovate, innovate! Here comes American rebirth. In D. Araya & M. A. Peters (Eds.), *Education in the creative economy: Knowledge and learning in the age of innovation*. New York: Peter Lang.
Nederveen Pieterse, J. (2011). Global rebalancing: Crisis and east-south turn. *Development and Change*, 42(1), 22–48.
Nederveen Pieterse, J. (2012). Growth and social policies: Towards inclusive growth. *Briefing Policy Special Issue*. Retrieved from http://www.jannederveenpieterse.com/pdf/Growth_social_policies.pdf.

Nelson, R. R. (Ed.) (1993). *National innovation systems: A comparative analysis.* New York: Oxford University Press.
Newfield, C. (2008). *Unmaking the public university: The forty-year assault on the middle class.* Cambridge, MA: Harvard University Press.
Newman, J. (2001). *Modernising governance: New labour, policy and society.* London: Sage.
Nolan, M., & Pack, H. (2003). *Industrial policy in an era of globalization: Lessons from Asia.* Washington, DC: Peterson Institute.
Nonaka, I. (1991). The knowledge creating company. *Harvard Business Review,* 69(6), 96–104.
Obama, B. (2009, March 10). Remarks by the president to the Hispanic Chamber of Commerce on a complete and competitive American education. Speech presented at Washington Marriott Metro Center, Washington, DC. Retrieved from http://www.whitehouse.gov/the_press_office/Remarks-of-the-President-to-the-United-States-Hispanic-Chamber-of-Commerce.
OECD. (1996). *The knowledge-based economy.* Paris: OECD.
OECD. (1997). *Beyond 2000: The new social policy agenda.* OECD Working papers, vol. V, no. 43. Paris: OECD.
OECD. (2006). *Starting strong.* Paris: OECD.
OECD. (2007a). *Lifelong learning and human capital.* Paris: OECD.
OECD. (2007b). *Understanding the social outcomes of learning.* Paris: OECD.
OECD. (2007c). *Giving knowledge for free: The emergence of open educational resources.* Paris: OECD. Retrieved from http://www.oecd.org/dataoecd/35/7/38654317.pdf.
OECD (2008a). *Growing unequal.* Paris: OECD.
OECD (2008b). *Open educational resources: Opportunities and challenges.* Paris: OECD. Retrieved from http://www.oecd.org/edu/ceri/37351085.pdf.
OECD (2013a). *OECD skills outlook 2013: First results from the survey of adult skills.* Paris: OECD. Retrieved from http://skills.oecd.org/documents/OECD_Skills_Outlook_2013.pdf.
OECD (2013b). Building blocks for smart networks. *OECD Digital Economy Papers,* No. 215. Paris: OECD. Retrieved from http://www.oecd-ilibrary.org/science-and-technology/building-blocks-for-smart-networks_5k4dkhvnzv35-en.
Pages, E. (2010). Obama's innovation policy: Can the new direction hold? *Local Economy,* 25(8), 678–684.
Palley, T. (2011). The rise and fall of export-led growth. Working paper no. 675. Annandale-on-Hudson, NY: Levy Economics Institute. Retrieved from http://www.levyinstitute.org/pubs/wp_675.pdf.
Patel, P. and Pavitt, K. (1994). The nature and economic importance of national innovation systems. *Science, Technology and Industry Review,* (14), 9–32.
Perkins, D., Nelms, L., & Smyth, P. (2004). *Beyond neo-liberalism: The social investment state?* Social Policy Working Paper No. 3. Fitzroy: Brotherhood of St. Laurence. Retrieved from http://www.bsl.org.au/pdfs/beyond_neoliberalism_social_investment_state.pdf.

Peters, M. A. (2001). National education policy constructions of the "knowledge economy": Towards a critique. *Journal of Educational Enquiry, 2*(1), 1–22.
Peters, M. A. (2009a). Education, creativity and the economy of the passions. In M. A. Peters, S. Marginson, & P. Murphy (Eds.), *Creativity and the global knowledge economy*. New York: Peter Lang.
Peters, M. A. (2009b). Introduction: Knowledge goods, the primacy of ideas, and the economics of abundance. In M. A. Peters, S. Marginson, & P. Murphy (Eds.), *Creativity and the global knowledge economy*. New York: Peter Lang.
Peters, M. A. (2010). Three forms of the knowledge economy: Learning, creativity, and openness. *British Journal of Educational Studies, 58*(1), 67–88.
Peters, M. A. (2012). Greening the knowledge economy: A critique of neoliberalism. *Truthout*. Retrieved from http://truth-out.org/news/item/9642-greening-the-knowledge-economy-a-critique-of-neoliberalism?tmpl=component&print=1.
Piaget, J. (1954). *The construction of reality in a child*. New York: Basic Books.
Pierson, C. (2007). *Beyond the welfare state? The new political economy of Welfare*. University Park: Pennsylvania State University.
Piketty, T. (2014). *Capital in the twenty-first century*. Cambridge, MA: Harvard University Press.
Piketty, T., & Saez, E. (2012). *Optimal labor income taxation*. NBER Working Paper 18521. Cambridge, MA: National Bureau of Economic Research. Retrieved from http://www.nber.org/papers/w18521.
Pink, D. (2005). *A whole new mind: Moving from the information age to the conceptual age*. New York: Riverhead Books.
Polanyi, K. (1944). *The great transformation*. New York: Rinehart.
Ponniah, T. (2013, October 30). OECD skills outlook 2013: The skills needed for the 21st century. *Rabble*. Retrieved from http://rabble.ca/columnists/2013/10/oecd-skills-outlook-2013-skills-needed-21st-century.
Porat, M. (1977). *The information economy: Definition and measurement*. (U.S. Department of Commerce, Office of Telecommunications, US Government Printing Office Stock No. 003-000-00512-7). Washington, DC: US Government Printing Office.
Porter, M. E. (1990). *The competitive advantage of nations*. New York: Free Press.
Powell, W. W., & Snellman, K. (2004). The knowledge economy. *Annual Review of Sociology, 30*, 199–220.
Power, M. (1996). *The audit explosion*. London: Demos; White Dove Press.
Putnam, R. (2000). *Bowling alone: The collapse and revival of American community*. New York: Simon and Schuster.
Quah, D. (2003). Digital goods and the new economy. In Derek Jones (Ed.), *New economy handbook* (pp. 289–321). Amsterdam: Academic Press Elsevier Science.
Rae, D. (2010). Universities and enterprise education: Responding to the challenges of the new era. *Journal of Small Business and Enterprise Development, 17*(4), 591–606.
Ravitch, D. (2011). *The death and life of the great American school system: How testing and choice are undermining education*. New York: Basic Books.

Rifkin, J. (2011). *The third industrial revolution: How lateral power is transforming energy, the economy, and the world*. New York: Palgrave Macmillan.

Rifkin, J. (2014). *The zero marginal cost society: The Internet of things, the collaborative commons, and the eclipse of capitalism*. New York: Palgrave Macmillan.

Rizvi, F., & Lingard, B. (2010). *Globalizing education policy*. New York: Routledge.

Robinson, K. (2001). *Out of our minds: Learning to be creative*. Oxford: Capstone.

Romer, P. (1986). Increasing returns and long-run growth. *Journal of Political Economy*, *94*(5), 1002–1037.

Romer, P. (1990). Endogenous technological change. *Journal of Political Economy*, *98*(5), S71–S102.

Romer, P. (1994). The origins of endogenous growth. *Journal of Economic Perspectives*, *8*(1), 3–22.

Rothstein, R. (2008, April 7). "A nation at risk" twenty-five years later. CATO Unbound. Retrieved from http://www.cato-unbound.org/2008/04/07/richard-rothstein/nation-risk-twenty-five-years-later.

Rotman, D. (2013, June). Technology is destroying jobs. *MIT Technology Review*. Retrieved from http://www.technologyreview.com/featuredstory/515926/how-technology-is-destroying-jobs/.

Sahlberg, P. (2006). Education reform for raising economic competitiveness. *Journal of Educational Change*, *7*, 259–287.

Saltman, K. J. (2003). *The Edison schools: Corporate schooling and the assault on public education*. New York: Routledge

Saltman, K. J. (2007). *Capitalizing on disaster: Taking and breaking public schools*. Boulder, CO: Paradigm

Saltman, K. J. (2010a). Democratic education requires rejecting the new corporate two-tiered school system. *American Journal of Education*, *118*(3), 389–393.

Saltman, K. J. (2010b). *The gift of education: Public education and venture philanthropy*. New York: Palgrave Macmillan.

Sassen, S. (1991). *The global city: New York, London, Tokyo*. Princeton, NJ: Princeton University Press.

Saxenian, A. L. (2006). *The new argonauts: Regional advantage in a global economy*. Cambridge, MA: Harvard University Press.

Scardamalia, M. (2002). Collective cognitive responsibility for the advancement of knowledge. In B. Smith (Ed.), *Liberal education in a knowledge society* (pp. 67–98). Chicago: Open Court.

Schultz, T. W. (1961). Investment in human capital. *American Economic Review*, *51*(2), 1–17.

Schultz, T. W. (1964). Education and values conducive to economic growth. *Agricultural Policy Review*, *2*, 4–6.

Schultz, T. W. (1971). *Investment in human capital: The role of education and of research*. New York: Free Press.

Schumpeter, J. (1976 [1942]). *Capitalism, socialism and democracy*. New York: Harper & Row.

Scott, J. (2009). The politics of venture philanthropy in charter school policy and advocacy. *Educational Policy*, *23*(1), 106–136.

Shapiro, J. M. (2006). Smart cities: Quality of life, productivity, and the growth effects of human capital. *Review of Economics and Statistics, 88*(2), 324–335.
Selwyn, N. (2009). The "new" connectivities of digital education. In M. Apple, L. Armand Gandin, & S. Ball (Eds.), *International Handbook of the Sociology of Education*. London: Routledge.
Shirky, C. (2008). *Here comes everybody: The power of organizing without organizations*. New York: Penguin.
Siemens, G. (2005). Connectivism: A learning theory for the digital age. *International Journal of Instructional Technology and Distance Learning, 2*(1), 3–10.
Sklair, L. (2001). *The transnational capitalist class*. Oxford: Wiley-Blackwell.
Slaughter, A. M. (2004). *A new world order*. Princeton, NJ. Princeton University Press
Slaughter, S., & Leslie, L. (1997). *Academic capitalism: Politics, policies and the entrepreneurial university*. Baltimore, MD: Johns Hopkins University Press.
Slaughter, S., & Rhoades, G. (2004). *Academic capitalism and the new economy: Markets, state and higher education*. Baltimore, MD: Johns Hopkins University Press.
Smith, A. (1776). *An inquiry into the nature and causes of the wealth of nations*. London: W. Strahan.
Solow, R. M. (1957). Technical change and the aggregate production function. *Review of Economics and Statistics*. MIT Press, *39*(3), 312–320.
Spitz, A. (2004). Are skill requirements in the workplace rising? Stylized facts and evidence on skill-biased technological change. Centre for European Economic Research. Retrieved from ftp://ftp.zew.de/pub/zew-docs/dp/dp0433.pdf.
Spring, J. (2008). *The American school: A global context from the puritans to the Obama administration*. Boston, MA: McGraw Hill.
Stiglitz, J. (1999). Knowledge as a global public good. In I. Kaul, I. Grunberg, & M. A. Stern (Eds.), *Global public goods: International cooperation in the 21st century* (pp. 308–325). New York: Oxford University Press.
Tapscott, D. (1997). *The digital economy: Promise and peril in the age of networked intelligence*. New York: McGraw-Hill.
Tapscott, D., & Williams, A. (2006). *Wikinomics: How mass collaboration changes everything*. New York: Portfolio.
Taylor-Gooby, P. (2008). The new welfare settlement in Europe. *European Societies, 10*(1), 3–24.
Toffler, A. (1980). *The third wave*. New York: Bantam.
Toffler, A. (1990). *Powershift*. New York: Bantam.
Touraine, A. (1971). *The post-industrial society. Tomorrow's social history: Classes, conflicts and culture in the programmed society*. New York: Random House.
Towse, R. (Ed.). (2005). *Handbook of Cultural Economics*. Cheltenham, UK: Edward Elgar.
Tyack, D., & Tobin, W. (1994). The "grammar" of schooling: Why has it been so hard to change? *American Educational Researcher, 31*(3), 453–480.
UN DESA. (2010). Progress to date and remaining gaps in the implementation of the outcomes of the major summits in the area of sustainable development, as well as an analysis of the themes of the conference. Report for the Preparatory Committee for the United Nations Conference on Sustainable Development.

New York: United Nations. Retrieved from http://www.uncsd2012.org/content/documents/N1030256.pdf.

UNCTAD. (2008). *The creative economy report 2009. The challenge of assessing the creative economy: Towards informed policy-making*. New York: United Nations. Retrieved from http://unctad.org/en/Docs/ditc20082ceroverview_en.pdf.

UNCTAD. (2009). *The information economy report 2009: Trends and outlook in turbulent times*. New York: United Nations. Retrieved from http://unctad.org/en/Docs/ier2009_en.pdf.

UNEP. (2014). *Measuring the environmental goods and services sector: Issues and challenges*. New York: UNEP. Retrieved from http://www.unep.org/greeneconomy/portals/88/documents/WorkingPaperEGSSWorkshop.pdf.

UNESCO. (2010). *Education for all global monitoring report: Reaching the marginalized*. Paris: UNESCO.

UNICEF. (2000). *The leagues table of child poverty in rich nations*. Florence: UNICEF Innocenti Research Centre.

US Congressional Budget Office. (2012). Actual ARRA spending over the 2009–2011 period quite close to CBO's original estimate. Retrieved from http://www.cbo.gov/publication/42682.

US Department of Education. (2009). The American recovery and reinvestment act of 2009: Saving and creating jobs and reforming education. Retrieved from http://www2.ed.gov/policy/gen/leg/recovery/implementation.html.

US Department of Education. (2010a). *A blueprint for reform: The reauthorization of the elementary and secondary education act*. Alexandria, VA: Education Publications. Retrieved from http://www2.ed.gov/policy/elsec/leg/blueprint/blueprint.pdf.

US Department of Education. (2010b). Research behind the Obama administration's proposal for reauthorizing the Elementary and Secondary Education Act (ESEA). Alexandria, VA: Education Publications. Retrieved from http://www.ed.gov/blog/2010/05/research-behind-the-obama-administration.

US Department of Education. (2010c). Transforming American education: Learning powered by technology. Washington, DC: US Department of Education, Office of Educational Technology. Retrieved from http://www.ed.gov/sites/default/files/netp2010.pdf.

US Department of Labor Statistics. (2013). Occupational employment projections to 2022. Retrieved from http://www.bls.gov/opub/mlr/2013/article/occupational-employment-projections-to-2022.htm.

Varela, F., Thomson, E., & Rosch, E. (1991). *The embodied mind: Cognitive science and human experience*. Cambridge, MA: MIT Press.

Venturelli, S. (2005). Culture and the creative economy in the information age. In J. Hartley (Ed.), *Creative industries* (pp. 391–398). Malden, MA: Blackwell.

Violante, G. L. (2014). Skill-biased technical change. *The new Palgrave dictionary of economics*. (2nd ed.). Steven N. Durlauf & Lawrence E. Blume (Eds.). Retrieved from http://www.dictionaryofeconomics.com/article?id=pde2008_S000493.

Von Hippel, E. (2005). *Democratizing innovation*. Cambridge, MA: MIT Press.

Vygotsky, L. S. (1978). *Mind in society: The development of higher psychological processes*. Cambridge, MA: Harvard University Press.

Waks, L. (2011). Transforming American education: Revolution or counter-revolution. *E-Learning and Digital Media, 8*(2), 145–153.
Waks, L. (2013). *Education 2.0: The learning web revolution and the transformation of the school.* New York: Paradigm Press.
Weber, M. (1978 [1922]). *Economy and society: An outline of interpretive sociology.* Berkeley: University of California Press.
Wheatley, M. (1998). What is our work? In L. Spears (Ed.), *Insights on leadership: Service, stewardship, spirit, and servant-leadership.* New York: John Wiley and Sons.
White House. (2011). *A strategy for American innovation: Securing our economic growth and prosperity.* Washington, DC: Executive Office of the President, National Economic Council, Office of Science and Technology Policy, The White House.
Widerquist, K., Noguera, J. A., Vanderborght, Y., & De Wispelaere, J. (Eds.). (2013). *Basic income: An anthology of contemporary research.* Chichester, UK: Wiley Blackwell.
Williamson, J. (1990). The progress of policy reform in Latin America. In J. Williamson, (Ed.), *Latin American adjustment: How much has happened.* Washington, DC: Institute for International Economics.
Wolfram, C. (2010). Moving to the computational knowledge economy. Retrieved from http://river-valley.zeeba.tv/moving-to-the-computational-knowledge-economy/.
World Bank. (2003). *Lifelong learning in the global knowledge economy: Challenges for developing countries.* Washington, DC: The World Bank.
World Bank. (2005). *Economic growth in the 1990s: Learning from a decade of reform.* Washington, DC: The World Bank.
World Bank. (2008a). *Global economic prospects 2008.* Washington DC: The World Bank.
World Bank (2008b). *The growth report: Strategies for sustained growth and inclusive development.* Washington, DC: The World Bank.
Yeaxlee, B. A. (1929). *Lifelong education.* London: Cassell.
Zhao, Y. (2009). *Catching up or leading the way: American education in the age of globalization.* Alexandria, VA: ASCD.
Zhao, Y. (2012a). Reforming Chinese education: What China is trying to learn from America. *Solutions, 2*(2), 38–43.
Zhao, Y. (2012b). *World class learners: Educating creative and entrepreneurial students.* Thousand Oaks, CA: Corwin.
Zoellick, R. (2010, April). The end of the third world? Modernizing multilateralism for a multipolar world. Speech to Woodrow Wilson Center for International Scholars (April 14). Retrieved from http://web.worldbank.org/WBSITE/EXTERNAL/NEWS/0,,contentMDK:22541126~pagePK:34370~piPK:42770~theSitePK:4607,00.html.
Zuboff, S. (1988). *In the age of the smart machine: The future of work and power.* New York: Basic Books.

# Index

Acemoglu, Daron, 138
Advanced Research Projects Agency Energy (ARPA-E), 42, 82
Affordable Care Act, 82
*The Age of Discontinuity* (Drucker), 31
America COMPETES Act, 42
American Opportunity Tax Credit, 84
American Recovery and Reinvestment Act (ARRA), 42, 85–7
Anglo-Saxon model of political economy, 20
anti-immigration policies, 157n4
Asia, 22, 36–7, 62–3
assessment, 24, 91–3, 95–6, 101
Autor, David H., 138

Basic Minimum Income (BMI), 150
Bauwens, Michel, 11, 56–7, 108, 117–23, 152–3
Bell, Daniel, 32, 33
Benkler, Yochai, 54–5, 56
"Big Data," 71
biosphere, 133
Blair, Tony, 49
*A Blueprint for Reform* (BFR), 90–9
bounded entrepreneurship, 26
BRIC countries (Brazil, Russia, India, China), 36, 37, 72. *See also* specific countries
Brinkman, Donald, 12, 108, 122, 124
Brynjolfsson, Erik, 3, 4, 38
Bush administration, 42
business theory of change, 118

Campbell, Tim, 72
"cancer phase" of capitalism, 66
Castells, Manuel, 54
charter schools, 89, 91, 118
China, 21, 36–7, 43, 63, 131
Cillers, Paul, 158n1
class (socioeconomic), 75, 79, 96–7
clean energy, 42, 129–30
climate change, 66–8, 130–2, 150
cloud computing, 71
cognitive capitalism, 119–20
Coleman Report, 23
Collins, John, 141–2
*The Coming of Postindustrial Society* (Bell), 32–3
Common Core State Standards Initiative (CCSSI), 88, 98, 101
commons-based peer production, 55, 58, 151
communities-of-practice, 27
community as curriculum, 120, 123, 133
copyright, 55, 59, 61
Cormier, David, 120, 123–4, 133
corporatization (of education), 117–18
creative class, 53, 64, 109, 127
Creative Commons licensing, 59
Creative Economy
  characteristics of, 53, 109
  creative industries, 62–4
  economic value of creativity, 64–6
  implications for educational reform, 128–9

Creative Economy—*Continued*
  intellectual property, 60–1
  as new form of capitalism, 124–8
  overlaps with other paradigms, 74–5
  creative industries, 62–3
  cultural industries, 62, 143
Cunningham, Stuart, 62

Darling-Hammond, Linda, 25, 40–1
Davidson, Cathy, 11, 108, 114–15
Department of Energy, 42
design (as intellectual property), 55
Dewey, John, 129
Dicken, Peter, 36–7, 43
digital Taylorism, 139
Drucker, Peter, 31, 33
Duncan, Arne, 88

education
  as cultural industry, 143
  as economic engine, 4, 9
  as human capital investment, 39
  income inequality and, 23, 40–1
education inequality, 112–13
education informatics, 141–3
educational attainment, 22, 23, 65
Elementary and Secondary Education Act (ESEA), 90
endogenous growth theory, 13, 18, 44
energy internet, 69
Engelbart, Douglas, 141
entrepreneurship, 26–7, 44, 82, 83, 84, 126
equipotency, 57
European Union, 47

factory schools, 6–7, 104
feudalism, economic, 40
financial crisis (2008), 45, 68, 85–6, 139, 145
"flat world," 64–5
flexicurity, 49
flexitronic model, 104

Florida, Richard, 11, 18, 64–5, 108, 124–8
Forum on the Impact of Open Courseware for Higher Education in Developing Countries, 58–9
four R's of openness, 59–60
France, 47
Free and Open Source Software (FOSS), 59
Freeman, Christopher, 44
Fukuyama, Francis, 145–6
funding, for education, 87, 89–90
futurology, 34

gaming, 142
Garrison, Jim, 19, 105
gated globalization, 43
Gates Foundation, 97–8
Germany, 47
Gibb, Allan, 27
Giddens, Anthony, 49
Gini coefficient, 40
globalization, 19–20, 36–7, 67
  gated, 43
Goldin, Claudia, 22, 23–4
government, role of. *See* State, role of
grammar of schooling, 7
Great Recession. *See* financial crisis (2008)
Green Economy
  ARRA investments, 42
  characteristics of, 53, 66–7, 109
  democratic nature of, 70, 73–4
  implications for educational reform, 132–3
  infrastructure, 69–71
  innovation in, 129–33
  overlaps with other paradigms, 74–5
  public policy and, 67–9
  smart cities, 71–3
green jobs, 67
Green New Deal, 67

Hall, Peter A., 12
Hardt, Michael, 120
Head Start, 84
Health Care and Education Reconciliation Act, 84
Hemerijck, Anton, 28, 48, 148
Hilton, John, 59–60
Hobsbawm, Eric, 28
Hollands, Robert, 72
Howkins, John, 64
human capital
   Bauwens on, 120
   Creative Economy and, 127, 128–9
   decline in quality, 138
human capital development, 49, 74–5, 110–17
human capital theory, 1, 17–18, 135, 144
human intelligence, augmentation of, 141–3

income inequality, 5, 23, 40–1, 145, 156n3
India, 111
information age, 32
information and communication technologies (ICTs)
   Bell on, 33
   Brynjolfsson and McAfee on, 3
   in Creative Economy discourse, 60, 61
   effect on knowledge labor, 139, 143
   in Green Economy (Rifkin), 69–71
   in Network Economy, 120, 151
   open education and, 59
   role in education, 7, 142, 143
   SBTC and, 1
   in smart cities, 72
information capitalism, 54
information economy, 32
information revolution, 32
innovation
   in Green Economy, 129–33
   Obama administration initiatives, 41–2, 79–84

innovation economics, 45–6
intellectual property
   in Creative Economy, 60–1
   global regulation of, 35
   in Network Economy, 55–6
   open educational resources, 59
intergrid, 68, 69, 70
International Labour Organization (ILO), 67
international tests, US performance on, 24
Internet of Things (IoT), 69, 71–2

Jenson, Jane, 48
job growth, 37
Jones, Van, 67

Katz, Lawrence F., 22, 23–4
Kelty, Christopher, 56
Kenway, Jane, 32
Kenworthy, Lane, 146
Kerr, Clark, 33
Keynes, John Maynard, 4, 134
Keynesian economics, 19–20, 28, 147, 148–9
knowledge, as public good, 55–6, 119, 151
knowledge capitalism, 32
Knowledge Commission, 111–12
Knowledge Economy (KE)
   Bauwens' rejection of, 119
   globalization and, 36–7
   market economy *vs.*, 124–5, 152
   multiple discourses of, 51, 52
   neoliberalism and, 8–9, 45–6, 47
   origins of, 31–3
   paradigms of, 8
   peaking of, 60
   as policy discourse, 33–5
knowledge society, 33, 54, 150–1
knowledge workers, 31, 33, 52, 119, 139
knowledge-based capital (KBC), 35
*The Knowledge-Based Economy* (OECD), 34, 35

knowledge-based labor, 3.
  *See also* knowledge workers
Kohlberg, Lawrence, 129
Kumashiro, Kevin, 96, 97
Kurzweil, Ray, 144

laboratory science, 151–2
Lingard, Bob, 14
Lisbon Agenda, 47
List, Friedrich, 44
Lundvall, Bengt-Åke, 43–4, 149

machine-to-machine (M2M) communication, 71
Machlup, Fritz, 33
Marber, Peter, 40
market economy, 124–5, 152–3
market promotion, 82–3
Marx, Karl, 58, 126, 150
massive open online courses (MOOCs), 144
Masuda, Yoneji, 33
Mathis, William J., 99
Mazzucato, Mariana, 46
McAfee, Andrew, 3, 38
McMurtry, John, 67
McNeely, Ian F., 143, 151
Means, Alex, 128, 140
Mellander, Charlotta, 18
Milani, Brian, 73–4
Montessori, Maria, 129
Moore's Law, 5, 152
Moravec's paradox, 3

*A Nation at Risk: The Imperative for Education Reform* (ANAR), 22–3
National Commission on Excellence in Education, 23
National Defense Education Act, 23
National Education Technology Plan (NETP), 100–4, 142
National Innovation Council, 111
national innovation system (NIS), 40–4, 46, 47, 78

Nederveen Pieterse, Jan, 34–5
Negri, Antonio, 120
neoclassical economic theory, 18
neoliberal capitalism, 119
Neoliberal Knowledge Economy
  characteristics of, 53, 109
  human capital and, 110–14
  implications for educational reform, 114–17
neoliberalism
  education policy initiatives, 14
  role of State, 45
  social investment theory vs, 47–9, 148
  social policies, 19–20, 39
Network Economy
  characteristics of, 53, 109
  democratic nature of, 57
  implications for educational reform, 122–4
  intellectual property, 55–6
  overlaps with other paradigms, 75
  rise of, 54–5
  social benefits of, 119–22
network society, 54
New Growth Theory, 17–18
newly-industrialized economies (NIEs), 21, 37
No Child Left Behind Act (NCLB), 23, 91
Nordic countries, 26, 48

Obama, Barack, 87–8
Obama administration
  *A Blueprint for Reform* (BFR), 90–9
  energy policy, 130
  green energy policies, 68
  National Education Technology Plan (NETP), 100–4, 142
  national innovation policy, 41–2, 79–84
  nationalization of education, 112
  policy documents, 10

Race To The Top (RTTT), 84, 89
response to labor mechanization, 144
response to SBTC, 140
*A Strategy for American Innovation*, 41–2, 79–84
technology investment, 37
open access publishing (OA), 58, 59
open education (OE), 58–60
open educational resources (OER), 58–9, 101, 124. *See also* massive open online courses (MOOCs)
open source movement (OSM), 55, 122
openness, four R's of, 59–60
Orsi, Cosma, 152

paradigms (of Knowledge Economy)
  overlaps between, 74–6
  summarized, 8, 53, 109
Partner State, 152
patents, 35, 55
peer-to-peer (P2P) production, 56–7, 69, 120–1
Pell grants, 84, 87
Peters, Michael, 31, 34
Petty, William, 17
Piaget, John, 129
Pink, Daniel H., 60
Pitroda, Sam, 11, 108, 111–12
positive welfare, 49
Powell, Walter W., 35
private-sector reform groups, 97
privatization (of education), 25
Program for International Student Assessment (PISA), 24, 104, 140
public good, knowledge as, 55–6, 119, 151
public knowledge building, 144

qualitative development, 73
qualitative research, value of, 12

Race To The Top (RTTT), 84, 89
Rae, David, 26, 45
Ravitch, Diane, 98

Reagan, Ronald, 20, 145
recursive public, 56
Research and Experimentation Tax Credits, 82
rhizomatic model, 120, 123
Rifkin, Jeremy, 5–6, 68, 69–70, 132–3, 152
Rizvi, Fazal, 14
Romer, Paul M., 17–18

Saltman, Kenneth J., 96
Sandia Report, 23
Schumpeter, Joseph, 44, 45, 126
science, technology, engineering and math (STEM)
  Bush administration policies, 42
  KE view of, 110–11
  in NETP, 101
  Obama administration on, 21
  professions forecast, 140–1
  Rifkin on, 5
  in SAI, 81–2, 83–4
Seba, Tony, 12, 110, 112–13, 129–31
*The Second Machine Age* (Brynjolfsson and McAfee), 3
self-directed learning, 27
skill-biased technological change (SBTC), 1, 18, 140
smart cities, 71–3
smart grid, 67–70, 130
smart systems, 71–2
smart technologies, 71
smiling curve, 2
Smith, Adam, 17
Snellman, Kaisa, 35
social inequality, 39
social investment theory, 47–9, 146–51, 157n11
social market capitalism, 47
spending per student, K-12, 102
stagflation, 19, 20
standardized testing, 24–5, 104
standards-based reform, 91–2
Startup America, 82

State, role of
  in China, 43
  in education, 78–9, 140
  in innovation (see *A Strategy for American Innovation* (WH, 2011))
  in political economy models, 147
  in United States, 45–6
State entrepreneurship, 83
Stiglitz, Joseph E., 55
stimulus spending, 68, 89, 130
  American Recovery and Reinvestment Act (ARRA), 42, 85–7
  Troubled Asset Relief Program (TARP), 85
*A Strategy for American Innovation* (SAI), 41–2, 79–84
supply and demand (of/for knowledge), 55–6

Task Force on Skills for America's Future, 84
teacher unions, 118
teachers
  academic caliber of, 40–1
  BFR treatment of, 92–3, 96
  changing role of, 117
  NTEP treatment of, 101
  standardized testing as evaluation of, 115
  support for reform, 89–90
technological unemployment, 3, 4, 134, 139–40, 144, 149
Thatcher, Margaret, 20, 145
thick profits, 1–2
*The Third Industrial Revolution* (Rifkin), 68–70
Third Way, 49

Tobin, William, 7
Touraine, Alain, 33
Trade Adjustment Act, 84
trademarks, 55
*Transforming American Education: Learning Powered by Technology.* See National Education Technology Plan (NETP)
Trends in International Mathematics and Science Study (TIMSS), 104, 140
Troubled Asset Relief Program (TARP), 85
Tyack, David, 7

UNCTAD, 63
underemployment, 2, 114, 134
unemployment, 37–9, 49, 85, 114, 147. *See also* technological unemployment
Unified National Smart Grid, 68–9, 130
United Kingdom, 49
urban economies, 65–6
urban population, 64–5

Venturelli, Shalini, 60–1

Wagner, Tony, 12, 110, 113–14, 115–17, 118
Waks, Leonard J., 6–7, 103, 142
*The Wealth of Networks* (Benkler), 55
Weiner, Sharon, 141–2
welfare state, 19, 28–9, 47, 48–9, 147, 148
Welner, Kevin G., 99
Wolverton, Lisa, 143, 151
women, in labor force, 48

Zhao, Yong, 38–9

GPSR Compliance

The European Union's (EU) General Product Safety Regulation (GPSR) is a set of rules that requires consumer products to be safe and our obligations to ensure this.

If you have any concerns about our products, you can contact us on

ProductSafety@springernature.com

In case Publisher is established outside the EU, the EU authorized representative is:

Springer Nature Customer Service Center GmbH
Europaplatz 3
69115 Heidelberg, Germany

www.ingramcontent.com/pod-product-compliance
Lightning Source LLC
LaVergne TN
LVHW051912060526
838200LV00004B/102